Fathers and daughters

Sue Sharpe

London and New York

First published 1994
by Routledge
11 New Fetter Lane, London EC4P 4EE

Simultaneously published in the USA and Canada
by Routledge
29 West 35th Street, New York, NY 10001

Typeset in Times by J&L Composition Ltd, Filey, North Yorkshire

Printed and bound in Great Britain by
Mackays of Chatham PLC, Chatham, Kent

British Library Cataloguing in Publication Data
A catalogue record for this book is available from the British
Library.

Library of Congress Cataloging in Publication Data
Sharpe, Sue, 1945–
    Fathers and daughters/Sue Sharpe.
        p.   cm.—(Male orders)
    Includes bibliographical references and index.
    1. Fathers and daughters.   I. Title.   II. Series.
    HQ755.85.S5   1993
    306.874′2—dc20   93–24570

ISBN 0–415–10301–0
ISBN 0–415–10302–9 (pbk)

Contents

For my father

Acknowledgements

It is the feelings and experiences of fathers and daughters that form the basis of this book, and I would like to thank them all deeply for opening their lives to explore often painful and conflic-. ting aspects of the father–daughter relationship. I was always interested in the varying dynamics and characteristics of their relationships, and often very moved by events that had occurred within these. I identified strongly with many of their experiences and I hope that other men and women reading this will do so as well. I would very much like to thank Sandie Alden, Janet Holland, Anne Reid and members of the LIZAID group, for reading and commenting on some of my draft chapters; Sonia Lane for her invaluable help with transcription; and a special word of thanks to Jud Stone for her interest and encouragement, and for reading the whole manuscript.

Introduction

'As a man I have had a variety of relationships with women. I've had a wife, I've had a mother, I've had women friends, colleagues I've worked with, I've had a lover, but a daughter is something entirely different again. What you haven't had you don't miss but I'm aware now that I would have missed a great deal without a daughter in my life.'

Richard

'I believe that my relationship, or rather non-relationship with my father has had a profound effect on my ability to trust and relate to men in my adult life. As a child I wanted for nothing in the maternal affection sense, yet I had no affection from my father, nor would he join in games or any of the activities normally associated with parenthood. I think he cared about me in his own way but he never showed it. He seemed to believe that women were somehow inferior and I got no support from him when my own marriage broke up. When I hear other people talk of their close relationships with their fathers I feel I have really missed out on something.'

Jennie

Family relationships are by nature complicated, especially those between parents and children. While much has been talked and written about the relationship between mothers and daughters, that between fathers and daughters has received comparatively less attention, although it is equally complex and has as many significant consequences. It is also tempting to assume that fathering in general is a neglected subject, but this is not altogether true. As Lewis points out,[1] a number of accounts of fathering have been written during the last few decades, and each one similarly points out the previous paucity of work in the field and lays claim to be filling the gap. Much of what has been written about the father–child relationship comes from the United States.[2] The focus of such literature has tended to be the general role of fathers within the family. Where specific relationships with sons and daughters have been considered separately, it is usually in the context of sex-role development from a psychoanalytical, psychological or sociological perspective. In introducing a British anthology of women talking about their fathers in 1983, Ursula Owen[3] similarly questioned why there was so little work on fathers and daughters, and ten years later the situation has not significantly changed. One subject concerned with the father–daughter relationship that has, however, received attention in both the United States and Britain is the rise in reports of incest and other kinds of child abuse. This has stimulated research, literature and the establishment of advice agencies and helplines.

Why has there apparently been so much more research interest in mothering and the mother–daughter relationship than fathering and the father–daughter relationship? Or indeed the relationship between sons and their mothers and fathers? Certainly a major contributing factor in this is the view of the mother as being the more essential childcarer, with whom it was necessary for the child to make a satisfactory bond. This ideology fuelled the research literature on maternal deprivation. The relative importance of fathers and father deprivation received scant attention. In Western countries, the nuclear family structure is still taken as the basis of 'normal' family life, although the cracks are showing. Within this, the traditional domestic division of labour – in which fathers go out to work and mothers are responsible for home and children – still operates, even though many mothers now work part-time or full-time outside the home. Fathers retain the symbolic link with the outside world. The mother–child, and specifically the mother–daughter relationship is, however, still seen as a closer one than that of either daughters or sons with fathers, and one which is more accessible for the expression of emotions and feelings.

For a woman, the mother–daughter relationship represents continuity and 'sameness' while the father–daughter relationship represents a sense of 'otherness', and this is one of several factors which further complicate the father–daughter relationship. There is also a set of established rules and expectations around mothers and mothering which do not apply to fathers, and neither is there a fixed paternal equivalent. Parent–child relationships can prove a minefield to research, and with fathers, sexual taboos and the maintenance of emotional distance may have laid down mines that remain buried for many years. Sexuality overlays this subject with an uneasiness that is generally missing from mother–daughter relationships.

The role of the father as patriarch rests on a historical pedestal. Men, as fathers, are still identified with social, political and economic power, despite the significant inroads women have made this century. Supported by the continuing disparity in men and women's earning power (women in Britain earn approximately seventy-five per cent of men's earnings) fathers are identified with the more permanent provision of financial security, even in the face of visibly high levels of unemployment. Men are assumed to have an ignorance about and an optional role in childcare. A lone father tends to receive more admiration and attention than a lone mother, who is seen more as a social problem.

Where the nature of the father–daughter relationship has been explored or documented, it has been approached in various ways. From a psychoanalytic viewpoint, Freud's psychoanalytic theory of the Oedipus conflict (and its female parallel, the Electra complex) had its resolution in a girl's identification with her mother. The focus in Freud's theory and psychoanalytic theories which followed it was on the role of the father in the sexual development of the daughter. Fairy tales and other areas of Greek mythology have been employed to exemplify the nature of this relationship in some instances.[4] From a more general psychological perspective, the role of fathers has been included in child development, and involves exploring the effects of fathers on sex-role learning, achievement motivation, analytic ability, etc., as well as the possible implications of father loss and absence on their children. Most studies and discussions of the mother–daughter relationship also include some reference to fathers, however peripheral. Much of the work on this subject has been done by feminist writers and researchers who have been inspired to look more closely at the roots of their femininity and other aspects of development. Research into child abuse, as mentioned above, has also provided another focus for father–daughter relationships. From all these perspectives, research indicates that the father–daughter relationship has significant and far-reaching effects, and this is supported by the women and men whose experiences illustrate the following chapters.

This book is based mainly on interviews with or letters from daughters and fathers. Wherever possible I have tried to look at the relationship from both sides, unlike most approaches which focus on the daughter and the effects her father may have had on her development. Fathers have rarely been given the opportunity to voice their fathering experiences.[5] Some recent work in the United States that has addressed both sides of the relationship has done so by generating a range of categories into which daughters and fathers are fitted, such as competitive daughter, domineering father, etc. and defining possible outcomes from their inter-relationships. Particular attention is paid to the implications for a daughter's sexuality and her future relationships with men.[6] It is an appealing approach which documents a lot of information and research, and many of the pathways described make sensible and useful starting points, but such categorisation cannot help but be deterministic and ultimately over-simplistic. In this respect I was disappointed to find, for example, that my father and I could fit into several categories of relationship and I was not much enlightened, although cheered, to find I therefore qualified for a wide variety of possible outcomes and prospective partners. In real life, people elude tidy labels. Becoming aware of and understanding the nature and complexity of one's own parental relationship, however, does provide a starting point for change. Such knowledge can help women to start to take control of certain aspects of their lives which have been radically affected by their relationship with their fathers.

There are clearly many kinds of fathers, and many kinds of father–daughter relationships, which contain unresolved contradictions and ambivalence. The father–daughter relationship covers a sensitive and uneven terrain, where positive and negative characteristics can have a sometimes uncomfortable coexistence. This book explores the relationship at all ages. Daughters and fathers at different stages in their lives describe their feelings and experiences, for instance, in childhood and adolescence, in adulthood and old age. In the following pages various factors and processes operating in the relationships between fathers and their daughters are explored, using illustrations from both sides of this dynamic and comparing their perceptions and experiences where appropriate. Rather than impose a specific theory or fit people into categories, it seemed more appropriate to use a more open-ended approach that allows salient issues within the relationship to be voiced and explored by those experiencing them. I have chosen to highlight the aspects of the relationship which emerged most strongly from the daughters and fathers in my research. These are: early childhood experiences; approval and achievement; violence; sexuality; effects on future relationships with men; specific experiences of father absence, lone fathers and stepfathers; role reversal and dependency through ageing. The issue of sexual abuse has been but touched on in this book, since it is well researched and written up elsewhere and I have preferred to concentrate on other aspects of the relationship.

In researching for this book I talked to or exchanged letters with fathers and daughters from a variety of geographical locations and social backgrounds. They were contacted partly through advertising in newspapers, and partly through other sources and networks. There was a large response from women, of whom ultimately over forty were included, and for half of these I carried out interviews with their fathers. I also corresponded with a large number of daughters, and a few fathers, who wrote in detail about their lives and relationships. There was a variety of reasons for the father–daughter inbalance: many fathers I could not meet since they were unavailable at the time; or the negative or otherwise sensitive nature of the father–daughter relationship made meeting me inappropriate; or they were ill or no longer alive. Some of these daughters and their fathers were both working class: some were working-class fathers whose daughters had moved into middle-class jobs or careers through education; and others were fathers and daughters who were both middle class in occupation. A minority were from Asian, Greek-Cypriot and Afro-Caribbean backgrounds: the majority were white. They came from various parts of Britain: most daughters lived in a different area of the country from their parents, reflecting the relative ease of social and geographical mobility today. A wide age range was covered, from a young father in his twenties with a five-year-old daughter through to women in their fifties and sixties whose fathers were in their seventies or eighties. Their voices are heard throughout the book, becoming familiar to the reader through their contributions to many chapters. All the names have been changed to preserve anonymity.

There are significantly more women than men in this book and this is because daughters responded more enthusiastically to the opportunity of participating than fathers. As a result of one of my newspaper advertisements, I received nearly 150 letters, and over ninety per cent of them were from women. It was not unexpected to find that women were more open and articulate about discussing their relationship with their fathers than men were regarding their daughters. It seems to be women who are willing to respond to requests like this, who are concerned with relationships and able to share their feelings and experiences with other people. Many men appear to have much less interest and motivation to do this.

It is not a surprise then to find a marked contrast between these daughters and fathers, in the ways that the daughters could describe their feelings and emotions and the amount of thought they had put into exploring and analysing their family relationships. They often made their fathers look relatively inarticulate. This is not to say that the men did not talk: on the contrary, many spoke at considerable length but they tended to talk either in a more distanced way, often intellectualising their feelings rather than really describing how they felt, or they avoided emotions and feelings altogether, preferring to list or outline events that had happened in their daughter's childhood or a later period of life. These men seemed to be ill at ease with emotions, especially their own. They did not or would not recognise them, or they quickly packed them away if they threatened to emerge. There were times in my interviews with fathers when I wanted to shake them and say 'Yes, but what did you actually feel like?'. I rarely felt like this when talking with their daughters. It is possible that these fathers were being more reserved talking with me because I was a woman, or because to show me their emotion was somehow a betrayal of the family's image, but I think this would be an over-simplification. I believe the relative ability to express feelings and emotions is a real difference between men and women, and is at least partly rooted in boys' early experiences of growing up and identifying with male images and the representation of masculinity, in which any vulnerability or displays of emotion (apart from at births, deaths and on the sports field) tend to be seen as weakness. In any event, as a complaint of daughters against fathers, it is raised by women throughout this book.

It is not possible to measure the quality of daughter–father relationships, nor to reliably predict their outcomes. This book does not seek to prescribe answers nor make glib general statements but to provide a guided journey through a range of real life father–daughter experiences, which illustrate specific areas of interest or conflict and can provide a framework within which to explore and question our own relationships.

Chapter 1

Little girls

'As she grew older I can recall feelings which I suppose I still hold, of protection, possibly over-protection, towards "my little girl"; rushing to hold her hand and steady her if she looked as if she might fall, for example. Whether I would act the same if she was a boy I don't know. I've always tried to avoid "gender stereotyping", but subconsciously I don't think I expect her to be as physical or as sporty, nor do I push her to be so.'

Patrick

'I remember my dad buying me cars and things deliberately because I was a girl; probably if I was a boy he'd have bought me dolls and things!'

Sophie

'He's never made a difference between the girls and the boys of the family. The boys used to take turns at doing the dishes, in fact they were better at it . . . but I don't think he would have expected us to do the wallpapering or anything, whereas I probably would have made a better job than my brothers. He would say, "I need the boys for that"'.

Jean

The prospect of having a baby affects men in a variety of ways. Some are overjoyed; others are doubtful and nervous about their capacity for this role; and some give it little serious thought until it happens. Over the past few decades the traditional image and reality of being a father has, to some extent, been modified. Expectations have been created in which housework and childcare potentially are shared between men and women in the family, and there is an assumption that people have become more open about sexuality and the process of giving birth.

Men who became fathers several decades ago often had quite different expectations and experiences from those of young fathers today. David, for instance, is a journalist in his mid-sixties who has several grown-up children as a result of three marriages. He is typical of many fathers who have found themselves having children simply as an extension of marriage, because this was the next and appropriate thing to do:

'I became a father when I was twenty-five. I had an idea of being a father – you got married and so you would be a father, but if it were left to me, like many men, I think I would have put off having children until I was about forty. I think most men have a picture of being a father of a seven or eight-year-old boy to take out fishing or to football matches, whether they ever do that, it's a kind of myth. But babies – men want children but they don't want babies!'

Whatever feelings men have beforehand, having a child significantly changes the course of their lives. Peter is a building maintenance worker, a single parent in his late thirties, who has shared the responsibility for his fourteen-year-old daughter Melanie all her life, and especially since his relationship with her mother broke down when she was a few years old. His early experience was shared living in communal housing with his partner and daughter but now he lives on his own and his daughter joins him every alternate week. Recalling the time leading up to her birth, he said:

'I didn't think about it very much, but I felt very excited about it. I didn't really see or perceive what it meant, you only have short-term vision when you're twenty-four. In reality it means you're going to have care and control and emotional involvement for the rest of your life.'

Some fathers are extremely dubious about parenthood, questioning the sort of world they may be bringing children into. One of these I spoke to is Richard, whose early life as a technical representative had been transformed in his forties through getting a place to study history at university. He and his wife and daughter Sophie lived together in a remote part of the west country until Sophie went recently to college. Richard's experiences were also tempered by his earlier experience of childcare:

'I was very taken aback and very anxious when Pam became pregnant. We had in fact brought up my brother's boy for about five years. He proved to be a very difficult child and it was totally unrewarding; there was never any feedback at all.'

Whatever the initial feelings, these can all change when the baby is born, and men are confronted with this small but very real person, as Richard had found: 'When Sophie arrived the qualms did disappear and the angst slowly melted away.'

One thing men cannot do is give birth, and many are thankful to be missing this momentous but often very painful experience. In earlier years it was not the custom for fathers to be present at the birth of their children. It was discouraged by doctors and other hospital staff because men got in the way, their presence was unhygienic, they might faint at the sight of blood and at that time many men and women assumed it was inappropriate. In my parents' generation, the prospective father was hustled out and expected to wait in another room, or was called at work at some time afterwards with the message: 'You've just had a baby girl/boy'. My own father was hard at work at the office when he received the call from the nursing home that my older brother had been born. He was so excited that he fell off his bike on the way home.

Although today it is quite common practice for men to be present at the birth of their children, Richard remembers the day nineteen years ago his wife had Sophie: 'I wasn't actually there when Sophie was born, although I saw her quite early on. But to be truthful, it hadn't really occurred to me to actually be present at the birth.' In contrast, Malcolm, a freelance writer, had very much wanted to attend the birth of his daughter Anna, thirteen years ago, but had not anticipated taking an active part in it. However, because another mother was giving birth at the same time as his wife Claire, this caused a sudden shortage of nursing staff: 'I was like the assistant midwife, very much involved and really delighted. The fact that I was actually taking part was really exciting because it meant that it was our child and not just Claire's, because I'd been there. And when I saw Anna I felt fantastic.'

Obviously, having children can radically affect men's lives, both practically and emotionally, and the amount of participation that a father feels in the actual birth process can intensify his feelings of involvement. This in itself may not affect the later relationship between father and daughter, but it can add to the amount of personal investment in fathering that a man is already bringing to this role in his life.

For Tony, who works as an electricity board officer and lives with his wife and two teenage children in the north of England, it was a very significant moment in his life when his son Martin was born eighteen years ago, as he describes:

'I was there at the birth and I recognised then that my life had changed. We'd been married a couple of years before Martin came along – he was planned – and the emotion was enormous. In those first seconds when he was born, his life – or was it my life – flashed through my mind. Complete identity, change of direction. I was no longer a single man with a wife. I was responsible for somebody, for their life. It just changed and I knew it did. Fantastic. Laura was also planned, but having experienced Martin being born and all the emotion, then when Laura was born I didn't have the same experience. I didn't have that same identity, because as a man I didn't know what being a girl meant. I knew what being a boy meant, I'd been through it. I looked at her and I thought, that's nice, very nice, but it wasn't until she got to nine months that she had a character, and certainly by the time she was twelve months. But I couldn't get that kind of identity until that age.'

Having Laura was clearly different for Tony from having Martin in terms of his shared identification with the 'masculine' future in store for his son. While women have a shared identification with their daughters, some researchers contend that mothers tend to treat babies and young children of both sexes more similarly than fathers do.[1] Men appear to place a sense of being 'other' on their daughters more than mothers do on their sons. In his study of one hundred first-time fathers, Brian Jackson noticed that, although it is impossible to measure, the way fathers held sons and daughters at birth was different. He suggests that mothers hold more closely to both sexes, but that fathers tended to hold daughters more protectively close, while a male baby was held more at a distance and was gazed at more intensely.[2]

It seemed quite hard for men to put into words the nature of the different feelings they may have towards their sons and their daughters. Sean is a lecturer in his forties who is the father of a teenage son, two young daughters and a baby boy, in three separate relationships. He attempts to express what it feels like for him:

'I feel differently towards them in a very gut way. I don't think I love daughters or sons more than the other, but I have different feelings about them. I have no idea where that comes from, but daughter-ness is different from son-ness to me. I'm attracted by the femininity of daughters, wherever that comes from, whereas sons seem to offer a slightly different shared life with me. I'd play football with my daughters but I wouldn't look to them to be footballers, whereas I did a lot of training with my eldest son . . . while I say that, I'm aware my daughter is particularly athletic and that's something I'd like to develop. Even though I'm describing a different gut feeling towards them it wouldn't stop me giving her the same amount of time and attention on that. But the basic flush of emotion is slightly different towards her – I do find it a bit difficult to describe, the precise timbre of it.'

In looking at the ways that girls develop feminine identity and personality, it was suggested by Nancy Chodorow[3] that there is a kind of shared identification (or 'double identification') in which mothers identify with their daughters, having been daughters/girls themselves, and their daughters identify with their mothers through being of the same sex and often being involved more with their mothers and with other women in general. This may also occur with boys and their fathers, as Tony and Sean have described above, with their sons, although in the reverse direction. Some boys may find it less easy to identify with their fathers if they are not around in their lives very much, and consequently for young boys, their representation of masculinity may be partly formed by a rejection of femininity and anything seen as feminine. Fathers, like Tony and Sean, are therefore finding it difficult to identify with their daughters, as compared with their sons, because of their perceived differentness and the different future they anticipate for their daughters. There is already a psychological distance between them, created by this feeling of 'otherness'.

Some parents have definite ideas about whether they want a son or a daughter. It used to be thought more important to have at least one son in order to carry on the family line, and also to fulfil a romantic image of father and son sharing masculine activities together, playing or watching sport, or engaging in craft skills like carpentry. Having a son for purposes of inheritance or economic provider is not such a salient concern for many fathers in this country today, at least not in traditional English culture. In other cultures, such as Asian, having sons has much more significance.

Asian women's lower status is reflected in the relatively negative attitudes towards having daughters, reinforced by the greater cost incurred, since it is a girl's family that has to provide a dowry for each daughter on marriage. In postwar Britain, the middle-class ideal was to have one child of each sex, and advertisements portrayed a happy family as two smiling parents holding hands with their young son and daughter. Many men today would like to have a son but if they have one or several daughters instead, this is not usually a problem. Some even prefer it that way, like Raymond, for example, a self-employed businessman who is now in his late sixties. From a traditional Jewish family, he and his wife had two children, both girls, now grown up with children of their own. He says: 'I always prefer girls. I thought they were less trouble I suppose, and because boys are a little bit mischevious and I haven't got a lot of patience.' The idea that girls are easier to manage is a legacy from the traditional feminine stereotype and is not substantiated in general practice. Although I heard more young daughters described as being 'no trouble at all' compared to sons, a lot of other parents described many of the problems they have trying to communicate with, or control the behaviour of their teenage daughters.

Some men specifically profess to prefer women to men in general, and for them, the obvious choice is to hope to have a daughter. Several of the fathers quoted above took this view, like Richard for instance:

'I was very pleased I had a daughter, and also there's the underlying thing that in general I do, with a few exceptions, find women much more interesting than men. I've never been one of the boys.'

Malcolm is another who is happy to have had a daughter, and for him, females are definitely better:

'I just wanted a child with all four limbs in place, but I must confess I was delighted when it was a girl. I think girls are nicer than boys. I honestly don't know why, I just do like girls better than boys and women better than men.'

David, now an elderly grandfather, was not at all worried when he had four daughters before having a son:

'I didn't mind not having a son and having a lot of daughters. I can honestly say I had no interest in that aspect at all. I love

women. I like their feeling how they won't stand bullshit and
nonsense. And they're not bullying, they're more easily turned
into a jolly, laughing mood. It's much harder to do that with boys.'

I am perhaps tempted to agree with men who profess to think
women better than men, and that women are generally better
company, more sympathetic and usually more intelligent than
men, but I find this attitude in men sometimes a little suspect. Why
do men who so much prefer women's company to men's often
have few male friends? It may be illuminating to look back to their
own family and childhood and to their relationships with their
mothers or sisters. While some men's liking for female company
is genuine, I believe for others it can mask an underlying misogyny
and a desire to constantly prove they can exert power and control
over women. They use women as confidantes because women
understand feelings and are more emotionally empathetic; talking
to them is less exposing and threatening, and it can also serve to
enhance their ego. For fathers who use their children as extensions
of themselves, girls may serve a similar decorative role. Being seen
with an attractive teenage daughter may help to prop up her
middle-aged father's self-image, and detract from his own declining
sexual attractiveness and his conflict with the ageing process.

Men's primary role has traditionally been seen as going out to
work while women's role has been to stay at home and look after
the home and family. Such a rigid division may seem old-fashioned
to many young people growing up today, but it is not so long ago
that this over-simplification of real life was taken for granted (at
least amongst large sections of the middle-class population) and it
has not totally changed. It did ring true in describing the situation
for many fathers whose daughters were born just after the Second
World War, such as Raymond (quoted above) and his daughter
Margaret, now in her thirties with children of her own. Raymond
describes how he had little involvement in the care of his two
daughters:

'I did nothing at all in the domestic field. I used to go up to London
about seven in the morning and I rarely got back before half past
eight at night; they were always in bed. One of the things I regret
is not having a more active part in their young days. I probably
didn't play with them as much as most fathers as I had my own
business, I very often worked weekends as well. There were never
any problems, they always took to me very well. I would take

them places, but very rarely on my own, we would go as a family.'

Men's involvement in childcare and children's activities in general were not seen as crucial to the child's 'healthy' development, and in the 1950s and 1960s, for example, researchers on maternal deprivation neglected any possible significance of the father in family life and on children's bonding processes.[4]

Fathers from Raymond's generation tended to come home from work in the evening in time to play with their children for a short while, maybe even give them a bath, perhaps read them a story or put them to bed. There were of course exceptions, but this was what happened in the majority of families where fathers had employment and it is not so different from many families today. Margaret recalls her memories of Raymond from about thirty years ago when she was a small girl:

'My dad used to work in London so he used to commute. He had kippers for breakfast. I remember hoping he hadn't time to finish his kippers properly before he went for his train so I could finish them. If he got back in the evenings before I went to bed it was very special, his coming home was absolutely a big deal.'

Fathers took more of a recreational role with the children, as many still do today, which reinforces the different style of relationship that fathers and mothers often have wth their children. Tony, quoted earlier, has a fifteen-year-old daughter Laura, who recalls the fun she and her brother enjoyed out with her father, while her mother was doing things at home:

'My father's always been playful and jokey. He used to play with us for ages, it was really nice. It used to be Sundays. Mum would be cooking the dinner so me, my dad, and Martin would go up to the hills. It would be brilliant, we'd come back covered in muck. And he used to excel himself on holidays, he'd never stop making a fool of himself, and he'd always be laughing and throwing us around, really good fun.'

Fathers also took a more authoritarian role in which, although they were often absent at work for most of the day, they were given ultimate power over discipline and authority within the family, and held up as a threat to misbehaving children ('Wait until your father gets home!'). Fathers in this role become 'special' through their relative absence from day to day activities and trivialities. This contributes to the sense in which fathers and their love and support are not taken for granted in the same way as that of mothers.

Since the late 1960s, increasing liberalism, feminist consciousness and a greater focus on equality have chipped away at people's attitudes towards separate gender roles. The promoting of shared childcare was an important part of this, which meant both sexes taking an active part in the daily care of their children. Unfortunately, changes like these are hard to implement. The way that society is still structured and organised has meant that in general men earn more than women despite equal pay legislation; and a consistent lack of adequate childcare facilities has ensured that many mothers who would like to work continue to be at home. Although during the last two decades many more women than ever before have gone out to work full-time or part-time, whether through necessity or choice or both, the majority of women as mothers still hold the ultimate responsibility for the day-to-day running of the family.

Men have made relatively little progress in this direction, although in the 1980s the concept of the 'new man' came into being. This illusionary figure is someone who is not a nasty macho; he is softer, more considerate, shares housework and childcare and talks about his feelings and emotions. But however admirable the sensitivity and sharing qualities of this new man may be, unfortunately he remains a rare breed, and for the most part he has been artificially created and promoted by newspapers and magazines. (Some media sources would now claim that the new man is being transformed into the 'new lad', replacing the rather wimpy image that became attached to the new man by adding and reasserting some more macho activities.) Clearly, a significant number of so-called new men are in fact the old wolves in sheep's clothing, and the new lad is hardly worth knowing in terms of genuine equality. Of course, sharing, caring and sensitive men do exist: and there are now more men who share a bit, who talk about their feelings a bit, and many young men are growing up with more egalitarian assumptions about relationships and family life than their fathers. But they are a small minority, because the social structure still does not allow them to do this even if they want to; or they don't really want the implications of quite that much equal responsibility. Despite some progress, equality still remains somewhere on the distant horizon.

The type of childcare activities that fathers have traditionally been involved with include bathing, playing and taking children out, rather than the nitty-gritty activities of changing and washing nappies and other clothes, preparing food and administering meals. In the late 1970s, when I was researching for a book on working mothers,[5] women often commented that their husbands might look after the children but they refused to change dirty nappies. Luckily for men, the increasing use of disposable nappies has coincidentally relieved their distaste for this kind of task. Nowadays, more fathers do share these aspects of childcare,[6] both through necessity while mothers are out at work, and also because some men want to participate for themselves. The importance of fathers in children's lives has slowly been recognised and it is now considered desirable that men have more contact with young children in order to foster mutually closer and beneficial relationships. Young men today are growing up with an increased awareness of domestic equality as an issue, whatever the reality in their own homes, and young women take it as given (teenage girls I recently talked to in schools were adamant about this[7]), however much this may or may not be realised in their own future families.

Some working couples make specific efforts to share childcare and in areas of unemployment men may find themselves participating in childcare whether they wish to or not. Where couples have divorced or separated, single-parent fathers may also have sole or shared responsibility for the care of their children. Neil is a single father in his late twenties who has recently become responsible for most of the care of his five-year-old daughter Emily and his three-year-old son. He has achieved this through doing private tuition in the evenings, which leaves the daytime free for childcare. He and his partner Teresa had subscribed to a shared ideology of childcare and he looks back to earlier experiences before the separation:

'As parents we shared equally in the incessant rounds of changing nappies, cradling, pushing prams, playing. I had the knack of being able to settle Emily when she was inconsolable by pacing up and down with her on my shoulder, often through the night. I feel she still recognises that steady gait of mine when I carry her now.

'One major difference was that Teresa breastfed her for the first two years and that bliss I could never match. Because the breast was also a source of comfort as well as food there was a tendency to race to mum in distress. . . . But Freudian or not, there was something particularly close between me and Emily, which I could

– more prosaically – account for by the constant contact between us. In those days there seemed very few outside distractions and I veritably enjoyed latching into her awakening senses. I saw much less of my son during his first year and I regret it as it is only now that I have begun to have that intimacy, reciprocated, that I had with her. I don't think there was anything distinctive about her being a girl, on my part, in the closeness. It is only recently that I have seen her as a girl as distinct from a human child. Previously there was no difference in the clothes, the toys, the activities, etc. for either child, consciously at least. . . . Whatever sex stereotypes our children may have acquired, they do not involve who does the washing, cooking, cleaning, or who earns the money.'

Such consistent care and shared responsibility has helped to create a close bond between Neil and his daughter that is very valuable to him. Whatever happens to their relationship in the future, they have a closeness at this time that helps to remove the 'otherness' noted between some fathers and daughters. Clearly it is not just a one-way process we are concerned with here, in which fathers may affect their daughters in a variety of ways, but also the ways in which men themselves may be affected by their relationships and experiences with their own daughters.

As well as some changes in the nature of fathering, other aspects of men's and especially women's roles have changed radically over the course of this century. Greater equality has been achieved between men and women in education, work, sport, dress, etc. than there was some thirty or forty years ago. For instance, fashion changes promoting unisex items of clothing from Babygros and dungarees to the ubiquitous Levi jeans, almost unquestioned today, have all served to increase girls' sense of physical freedom and their ability to indulge in less traditionally feminine activities. Changes in employment patterns mean that while more women go out to work, more men also work from home or are unemployed.

In the 1970s and into the 1980s, feminists explored the ways that girls and boys are brought up in the family to be feminine or masculine and learn their appropriate sex roles and expectations: they seriously questioned the ways these are reinforced at school through the 'hidden curriculum' embedded in the education system; the discrepancies in pay and employment of men and women; and the ways male and female roles are represented in the media.[8] In all these areas, girls and women have been undervalued and discriminated against in some way. Girls and boys are channelled in different directions; and women's continuing responsibility for the family still places restrictions on them working or pursuing careers. The way children learn their appropriate gender roles begins in the family where differences are nurtured in the ways parents treat girls and boys, for instance, differences in the toys and games they are given; the tasks they are expected to do; the ways they are expected to behave. Some parents today have become aware of these issues and have changed their approach to children's upbringing and expectations, consciously encouraging the same qualities and behaviour in both sexes, but it is hard to make a lot of headway when society is still organised around many of the same separate principles.[9]

Fathers who are elderly now, look back to a time when gender roles were not such an issue. Stanley is a retired insurance agent in his seventies, who has always held stereotyped ideas about how girls and boys should behave. He has a son and a daughter, Rosemary, now in her late thirties. He and his daughter are both strong willed: Rosemary was often confounding his traditional image of femininity and they shared a close but frequently conflictive relationship during her childhood as Stanley recalled:

'Being an extrovert she was much more of a boy than her brother Mark was at a very young age. What does surprise me is how strong she was. Being a girl my idea has always been that a girl is the weaker sex. I did used to treat her more as a boy. I admire her for being strong willed, but sometimes it became very very frustrating. To me she was a girl, she shouldn't be strong willed. I expected her to be like a girl: meek and mild. This is the picture-book theory – little girl playing with dolls, does what she's told, but not Rosemary . . . I'd always play games with Mark far more than Rosemary. I'd expect him to play cricket and football, and Rosemary being a girl, she didn't come into it, not with the sports businesses, again that's the male ego. She'd want to play and I'd let her, but as she's a woman I thought she wouldn't be any good at it. But if Rosemary put her mind to something she'd do it, and she would invariably come out on top.'

In the family, girls and women nowadays are much more aware of sex discrimination than boys and men – and not surprisingly, as they are the recipients. Men prefer to remain ignorant if it means they have to share activities they would rather avoid, like housework. It is daughters like seventeen-year-old Michelle, for instance, who are trying to raise the consciousness of their fathers by pointing out some of the domestic inequalities still existing in the home. Michelle is still at school and lives at home with her parents in the east of England. She feels that although her father, a workshop manager in a garage, treats her and her younger brother equally in a lot of areas, certain things are still excluded:

'I don't feel he is totally fair. For instance, the washing up or preparing the table is often the cause of a row. I'm told more often than my brother to help and no reason is ever given, I'm just squashed if I try to bring up the fact he is being sexist.'

It is self-evident how and why it is always girls and women who change their expectations and aspirations, and who try to change those of men, who put up a predictable resistance.

Where there is only one parent taking all the domestic, financial and other family responsibilities, this may present a challenge to the stereotyped separation of sex roles and abilities. Perhaps less resistance may be found in one-parent families where daughters live solely or partly with their fathers. Here, family life is organised differently from that in a two-parent situation, or where children live solely with their mothers. Since her parents separated ten years before, fourteen-year-old Melanie has lived part of every week with her father, Peter (quoted early in this chapter), and the remaining part with her mother and her younger half-sister. Peter has cared for Melanie while she is with him and he does the general domestic work in their flat. He would like Melanie to share more in this now that she is older, and he also describes how he has tried to teach her some of the practical activities that interested him as a boy:

'I'm a maintenance worker so my bent is for mending things and building things and visualising drawing things out. I've given Melanie a lot of input on that, she really enjoys design, craft and technology stuff. I help her with that. And sporty stuff, football, tennis and stuff, I've encouraged her to play although I don't think she enjoys it now very much. She's done a few jobs with me, like putting up fences, things she really wants to come and do, she really likes . . . and she always gets the screwdriver out and fiddles around, she really likes that. Basically I've encouraged her throughout her life to be a tomboy. I've never pushed her into doing anything but I've shown her things that interested me when I was a boy so she might find them interesting, maybe games that boys play. . . . I suppose I taught her the boy folklore and she's decided whether she's interested in picking any of it up. I probably would have been one of those fathers taking their boys out fishing and stuff.'

Another such example of cross-roles can be found in Tom, a teacher who is also a single parent. He looks after his eleven-year-old daughter Kim and her fourteen-year-old sister Paula in London. Paula does not know her real father, who is still living in Trinidad. Tom is white and Paula's and Kim's mother is black. Their mother lives nearby with her new husband and baby daughter, and although Paula sees her fairly often she spends more time with Tom. She does many more activities with him than with her mother, and he has taught her various skills, as she describes:

'He's really into carpentry and woodwork, and I used to go into the shed and help him. Then he taught me how to make cakes as well. I still do carpentry, that got me into designing and stuff. Since then I've wanted to do something in carpentry. But my mum reckons I should be something like a midwife or a nurse. She reckons girls should be girls and boys should be boys. My dad thinks I should be whatever I want. Being brought up by my father has, actually, made me less feminine. At school I don't hang around with the girls at all. I'd rather play football or something like that. People accept that I'm a girl, but they act like I'm a boy. Dad encourages me to play football and things like that. At one time I was excluded from playing football in the boys' football team. Dad disagreed, so he came down to the school about it. He said I should play, so now I'm captain of the girls' football team. I think if I'd lived with my mum I would have been more into dresses and stuff. She's more for girls being girls. I feel sorry for my youngest sister when she gets older because she'll be a proper girl. Perhaps I should teach her that she can be a bit of a boy.'

These two single fathers have imparted a range of both 'feminine' and 'masculine' skills to their daughters. As neither has a son, it is not possible to see whether the same would happen in a mixed family of sons and daughters. The presence of a son may produce an increased awareness of potential gender-role differences that are then implicitly or explicitly reinforced in girls and boys. On the other hand, sons in single-father families may learn that it is usual and useful that men do the cooking, cleaning and other domestic work in the family. In general, the more experience people have and the skills they learn, the more self-confidence they can develop and, within the family, growing up and learning a variety of both feminine and masculine activities can contribute to this development. Fathers have an important role to play in the extent to which this happens.

It may be that fathers who only have daughters want to teach them some of the ('masculine') things that they themselves enjoyed doing when they were young, like Peter suggests above. John, however, provides an example of the opposite. He is an elderly father (aged seventy) who comes from a generation that assumed different aptitudes in girls and boys. He and his wife brought up their four daughters on a farm in the 1950s and 1960s. All his daughters are now married and his youngest, Barbara, is a teacher who now has a small daughter of her own. She recalls some of her father's attitudes within the family:

'I think he's very sexist so I think in subtle ways he didn't encourage us to do things men would do. I think if he'd had a boy he'd have expected him to learn everything he was doing on the farm. Whereas for me, I could put an undercoat of paint on or do things that didn't matter too much, but he didn't expect us to be able to do more and therefore we didn't think we could. If we had been very bold and said "I want to do the top coat!", I'm sure he would have let us, but I think we were all lacking in confidence. I think in subtle ways this might be something to do with his expectations, he would have expected a boy to do a lot more.'

Children are quick to pick up messages about what is expected from them, and how well they are assumed to be able to do different skills. This can significantly contribute to the development of confidence (or lack of it) in various areas of ability, usually traditionally practical, masculine abilities. This had been true for Sonia, a neighbourhood-development officer whose sixty-two-year old father still works as a self-employed painter and decorator. Now in her late thirties with young children, she has always been very proud of his practical talents but strongly regrets never having learnt them herself. She writes:

'I've always felt an admiration for my dad's practical capabilities . . . that "Dad will sort it out" has always been a source of security without doubt. But it is a source of sorrow to me that because I was a girl I never got taught the many practical skills which were potentially at my fingertips, quite the reverse. I still have a huge fear of machinery of any kind and I must also admit to a sense of dependency.'

Doing what are traditionally seen as 'masculine' (and therefore 'unfeminine') activities like climbing trees, getting dirty, playing football, helping to decorate the house, doing woodwork, etc., which usually earns girls the label of 'tomboy', extends the range of experiences for girls, and vice versa for boys. I hope that as the different expectations from girls and boys become less rigid, labels like tomboy and sissie may eventually become redundant, so that children will automatically do all sorts of activities, not just the ones seemingly appropriate for their gender. Parents in general, and men in particular, tend to be more concerned that boys develop masculine traits than they are that girls develop feminine ones. Therefore it is easier for men to accomodate to teaching girls to play football and put up shelves than it is for them to teach their sons needlework and cookery. They would not mind a daughter taking a carpentry set into school but would find it hard to let a son take in a sewing kit. The more masculine a father is, the more he will want men to be men and women to be women, and therefore try to enhance femininity in his own daughter.[10]

A significant number of the women I interviewed recalled being tomboys, and for several it was significant that their fathers had spent a lot of time with them doing 'masculine' activities. Other women also specifically mentioned that their fathers did not define or restrict them by virtue of their being girls, or that they consciously made sure that their daughters were included in everything. There are no hard and fast rules, as demonstrated by Rosemary's father Stanley (quoted earlier in this chapter) who had very stereotyped views and expectations about girls' roles, but he never made her feel that there were activities that she should not attempt because she was a girl. Rosemary comments:

'I didn't get any sense at all that he wished I'd been a boy. I think I was more of a boy in some respects than my brother was. I've always felt I was a lot physically stronger than him. So in a sense he got two boys. I used to help him a lot in the garden doing lots of physical labour. There wasn't ever any sense of "You shouldn't do that", and I very vividly remember helping my dad carry all the plants down to the new garden.'

Richard was quoted earlier on as being sceptical about having children, but his relationship with his only daughter Sophie demonstrates the possible rewards of trying to ensure that she felt she could succeed in anything she wanted. They have always spent a lot of time together, as he describes:

'From the time she was very small I believe that most of the activities I was involved in, she was involved in. What I tried to do was to expose her to as many things as possible. My perception is that she shared a lot of my time, a lot of the things I've done, even if it was simply working. For a period I was a technical rep. and she would come with me on holiday times and weekends . . . . I remember one time I took her to an air show and Pam, her mother, was horrified.'

Richard was determined that Sophie would become an able and independent young woman:

'There's something I call the "silly woman" syndrome, which is a tendency to say "I can't do that, that's man's work". All right, if it's shifting several hundredweight of coal but it may be mending a fuse. So I suppose I was unconsciously making an effort to ensure she didn't grow up to be what I call a silly woman. Wherever I could I shared whatever I had with her. Perhaps I could see a long-term return to me in that later she could share things with me, but also because I wanted her to take as broad a view of the world as possible. In terms of play, Pam took the major role, but Sophie used to play football with me and she played for the school football team.'

Their childhood relationship has been a close and caring one that has remained equally strong into adulthood and her father's attitudes and expectations for her have had a significant effect, as Sophie herself observes:

'We used to do things a lot as a family, going to the beach, and motor-cycle sports. We did it all together, I used to help my father to lapscore which I enjoyed. I wasn't very good at it but it made me feel like I was joining in. My dad's not somebody who feels that girls can't do things boys can. He's never treated me differently I don't think. Like I was taught to ride a motor bike – I wasn't a girl who was always climbing trees and things but I've always had this feeling that I'm not going to think I can't do something. It got to the stage when I was involved with Guides and Scouts and we used to go hiking and there was no way I'd ever admit I was tired. If the boys were climbing a tor in Dartmoor then I was going to as well. I think that was probably partly the way my dad treated me, never let me think I couldn't do it. He always has a go at everything and I think I do as well! I think he never really regretted the fact that he didn't have a son. I don't think he ever felt that as a girl I couldn't do anything . . . . My dad had an influence on me politically too, he made me very politically aware. I think he's given me a lot of my values. I tend to have a high opinion of learning, education's very good. I get that from both parents but particularly my dad. And much of what I do, hobbies and things, comes from what he instigated, like I'm still very involved in motor-cycle sport.'

It is clear that Sophie's development of confidence and self-esteem has been enhanced by her father's involvement and attitude to her upbringing.

In families like Sophie's where there is only one child, all the caring and interest is concentrated on that child, whatever their sex. If it is a daughter, some fathers may invest in her all the things they may have wanted for a son, and do the same 'boyish' activities with her that they would have done if she had been male. Lesley is another example. She is an only child, now in her late thirties. Her parents, Bob and Joan, were quite happy only to have one child, in fact, her mother had not really wanted children at all. Lesley and her parents did a lot of things together in her early childhood, when she developed a particularly strong relationship with her father:

'I think from the moment I could crawl or run around I used to be with my dad all the time. I'd be in the garden wherever he was, even if it was just sitting in the pram. Even when I was in my teens he'd be pointing walls and things like that and teach me how to do it. It was like he was teaching the son he didn't have . . . . I was a so-called tomboy when I was a kid. I just never ever played with dolls, that was boring. I used to play with cars. I had a railway track that dad actually built. Mum's always been very much into the housewife role, and dad sort of fitted into the usual man's role. I suppose I found it more exciting being with dad than with mum cooking and washing up. She used to be very jealous, very hurt, although I wasn't aware of it. I used to sit on dad's knee a lot.'

As Lesley became a teenager, her relationship with her father changed and she became much closer to her mother. This often happens as girls identify with aspects of feminine identity in adolescence which they share with their mothers, and confide more in her about things like periods and boyfriends. But for Lesley, this movement away from her father was also reinforced by the increasing disparity in their attitudes to women, race relations and other political issues that she felt deeply about. In her early twenties she became a lesbian, and she and her parents have maintained a strong and supportive relationship.

As only children, daughters like Sophie and Lesley appear to have benefited from the absence of brothers and enjoyed lots of things that might normally be seen as more appropriate for boys. A child having no brother but several sisters may be expected to reap similar benefits, but this was not the case with Barbara's experience. She has already described how she felt her father did not encourage her or her three sisters to do things he would have expected from a son, and she feels her life has been further restricted in that there were no boys' toys around, nor masculine activities to participate in when she was growing up, and she was very aware of being in a predominantly female environment:

'I think there's something very definite about a female atmosphere, I suppose quite unnatural really. I think I was a bit feeble through not having boys to toughen me up. There was a bitchiness and fighting amongst us, I suppose the atmosphere is a bit heavier with all girls around. I think it's a healthier atmosphere when it's mixed. And with our toys, I think it was more balanced on the side of female toys, it was very, very heavily balanced to female. I don't think consciously they tried to be sexist, it was more in unconscious ways.'

Her father, John, also expressed his awareness of the female nature of the household and was concerned that he had provided the only male role model for his daughters in the family. Sometimes he resented the lack of 'male' conversation in the home and the general emphasis on feminine things like cosmetics and fashion. Although John's and Barbara's experiences were obviously influenced by their being a family with four daughters and no sons, they were also a result of John's individual personality, his assumptions and expectations about the roles and behaviour of girls, and the lack of involvement in joint father–daughter activities. Little attention has been paid to the effects of a brother–sister relationship in the context of the father–daughter relationship. Girls may learn about male roles and identify with their fathers in some ways, but what might be the influence on their development of, for instance, a close and important relationship with an older brother?

Sometimes daughters and fathers develop a special relationship which may be closer than that between a daughter and her mother. As 'daddy's girl' they are mutually involved with one another, sometimes to the exclusion of other members of the family, including mothers. Girls in this position may use their little girl sweetness and charm to get their own way with their fathers. But as they get more mature, they have to separate from parents, develop identities of their own and be seen as individual adults in their own right. This can be hard for some fathers to recognise: they prefer to deny to themselves that their small daughters are really growing up and away from them and may no longer need them in the same way. It is also linked with fathers' problems in recognising daughters as growing into autonomous sexual beings (which is explored further in Chapter 4). Anne is single, thirty-one and still trying to separate herself from her father's concept and treatment of her as his young daughter. Treated as an only child from her father's second marriage, she and her father did everything together when she was small, as he worked shifts. He has never wanted to let her go and be independent, and although she has achieved well and has a good job, she finds it hard to break free:

'I'm still my dad's little girl, I think that's what I'm wrestling with and it's very much how my dad would talk about me, even now. He'd say I was his nipper. And if I say "Oh, dad . . ." he will say to me "But you'll always be my little girl." He sees me as an adult in some ways, like my work and my achievements, but on other levels he doesn't.'

Two of the older fathers described earlier also still think of their grown-up daughters as little girls. Raymond comments:

'Even today I cannot come to terms with the fact that they are women. I still look on them as my children. I look at them and I still say to myself "What I'm telling you is right", even though they'll tell me to my face "You're talking a load of rubbish". I want them to take the guidance from me, so I only look on them as children.'

Raymond thinks he would feel the same if his children were boys but, for most fathers with sons, their feelings of responsibility and protection are different and decline as boys grow into men. It is generally daughters who remain 'little girls' to their fathers much more than sons remain 'little boys'. Stanley has similar feelings about his daughter Rosemary:

'I still at times tend to try and dominate her which I shouldn't do, but to me she's still my daughter, she's still a little girl. Then I try to sort of wake up to the fact that she isn't a little girl any longer.'

Nevertheless, both these daughters (Margaret and Rosemary respectively, who have each had a close but resistant relationship with their fathers) have developed strong and independent personalities of their own.

Fathers can exert a strong influence on their daughters in childhood, and it may be they more than mothers who differentiate between the gender roles of their children. If men today are participating more in childcare, we could perhaps speculate that they might discriminate further between daughters and sons; on the other hand, their involvement in childcare may have the reverse effects on these kinds of attitudes and assumptions. In any event, it seems clear that the quality of the relationship a father has with his young daughter can play a vital role in helping her to develop confidence and independence, which she will take into other areas of her life.

Chapter 2

Approval and achievement

'I think me and my sisters were always terribly good, like we'd be terribly polite and eat everything, and go to bed when we were told. It feels like a lot of repression, a lot of pleasing other people. Nothing was quite good enough for my father. He wanted us to be more interesting, more outgoing.'

Fiona

'It always horrifies me to think of the power of people's personalities when you're young and closeted in a small world. So I don't really know how powerful my personality may have been and how much they may have thought they wanted to please me by being poets or politicians or something that they thought I wanted them to be. I suspect they may have wanted that. But I hate the thought of having influence on anybody except your free peers or equals. . . . If I faded out of the picture I'd really like it so that I didn't ruin everything. We're all going to fade out of the picture in the end. I think parents are too heavy a weight on children.'

David (Fiona's father)

The traditional feminine stereotype has been a predominantly passive one, in which girls are portrayed as quieter, neater, better behaved and more conforming than boys. There are undoubtedly a lot of girls for whom this does not apply but, nevertheless, there is a potential for these characteristics to develop, nurtured by girls' early experiences within the family. These are reinforced by the many images of women presented in the media which emphasise the importance of women making themselves attractive to please men, and they are present in women's traditional caring role within the family. Although gender stereotypes have been challenged and eroded to some extent over the last two decades, there are still significant differences in the ways boys and girls are treated within the family, at school, work and in other areas of life.

At a deeper psychological level, children identify with people who are close and important to them. Identification is not a simple process: they may identify with those they love or admire, or those who have power in their lives. Parents obviously play a crucial role, and children will identify with them differently depending on the type and quality of their relationships. For instance, a girl usually identifies with her mother, and takes on some of the characteristics appropriate to femininity and the feminine role. She may also identify strongly with her father and take on some of his attributes.

One personality characteristic that might be expected to be equally distributed between the sexes is the need for approval from other people. If you admire or care about someone, it is reasonable to wish to please them and earn their praise. This desire to please, however, seems to be a more female than male quality; the need for approval is one on which girls appear to be more dependent than boys. This can be seen as partly a consequence of the general role of women in relation to other people and especially to men; and a reflection of the greater power attributed to men in society in general, and over women in particular. One aspect of children's upbringing that may contribute to the development of this characteristic is parents' use of withdrawal of love and affection as a form of discipline. Therefore, if parents tend to discipline boys more by physical forms of punishment and use withdrawal of love and affection as a way of controlling girls, this may make girls more dependent on gaining approval and praise. If they do not receive the approval they seek, this further increases dependency and lack of confidence. Fortunately, there may be other important sources of approval available to replace this, but it may have consequences in girls' later relationships with men. From the experiences of many of the women speaking in this book, fathers are often unreasonably reluctant to give them adequate praise and approval, and whether or not this had radical consequences in their lives it remained a characteristic of their father–daughter relationships that was indelibly printed on their memories.

There are clear differences in the nature of the relationships that fathers and mothers tend to have with their children. It is generally mothers who are more supportive and nurturing and in whom children confide, while fathers tend to be concerned with more 'serious' issues like discipline, achievement and financial advice. In this context it is not surprising to find that many of the girls and women to whom I talked feel they have to prove themselves to their fathers, whereas a mother's approval could be (more or less taken for granted, like her love.[1] This may relate to their performance in school and through education; their choices and achievements in a job or career; their choice of partner in a relationship or marriage; or simply their conformity to some image that girls or women believe will please (or simply not anger or upset) their fathers. For example, Laura is in her fifth year of secondary school and lives with her parents and older brother. She has a good relationship with Tony, her father, and a secure family background in northern England. Getting the extent of approval she wanted from her father was something, however, that always seemed to elude her. She observed that her mother was better at telling her that she'd done well than her father was, and yet it is his praise that she values more:

'My mum's good like that . . . I think it's important that he's pleased with me or approves of me. It's nice, makes you feel good about yourself. More so than my mum I suppose, she's more like a friend. With my dad it's more like he'll only pay me a compliment if it's a difficult thing or I've done really well.'

There is an ironic logic in the fact that girls often seem to want to prove themselves more to their fathers than their mothers, yet it is their fathers who have most difficulty in granting them this approval.

Fathers' attention and approval is very important on many levels. Fiona is a twenty-eight-year-old mother of two young children. Her journalist father, David, talked in the previous chapter of his general lack of interest in having children and his preference for daughters over sons. He left Fiona's mother when the children (Fiona and her two older sisters) were young. Although Fiona visited David and his second wife regularly, she always found him distant and not sufficiently affectionate. She felt he held her at arm's length which made her nervous of him, wanting approval that he never gave but unsure of how to get it:

'He expected you to be very adult. He was very irritated by childlike behaviour: he'd never play just games, football or something like that, it would always have to be sort of cerebral. We used to play quotations and you'd panic because you didn't know one, you'd panic because it was too academic for you. . . . I wanted him to do things with me but because I didn't know him well, if he actually asked me to do something I'd be panicking. It'd all be like pressure, like you had to prove yourself. But he really didn't sort of listen to me. You knew there was something he was supposed to praise you for but you weren't quite sure how it was you were supposed to do it. He was never cross because you were naughty – because you never were naughty as you were so busy being good!'

The need for a father's approval exerts a powerful influence on daughters which can structure this and other personal relationships throughout women's lives. Fiona describes the way this need has affected her:

'My father is powerful and dominant, not in the sense of disciplinarian, but he was powerful in the sense that he was so appealing, so I hear this little voice in me always when I get in a new situation, like "Notice me, notice me, I am good aren't I? Did I do well for you? I laugh about it because I see it in everybody, it's obviously a really basic thing. I'm still like the nice little daughter. . . . I've got this thing that my father wasn't what I wanted him to be. I wanted someone who just thinks you're wonderful! Now it's part of my personality that I'd rather not try at something than try and fail, although whenever I've actually done something I actually do it quite well. I think it's being desperate to be approved of, but I don't think he'd ever really approve of anyone. He'll probably say "I think she's a brilliant person" and all this but there's part of me that just doesn't believe it – you're only saying that to be nice.'

The childhood relationship that David had with Fiona was powerful enough only to require a few words in terms of parental discipline, as she observes: 'He could really make me cringe. He never slapped us. It was just by some little phrase, I would be really hurt by it.' She also recognised that David was treating his small grandsons and granddaughters differently, and the girls were reacting in the same sort of way as she and her sisters had done:

'He was so different with my son to my sister's daughters, he was more physical. Meanwhile the girls were all doing what we did as girls, which is to sit on the edge and be very good and listen, not actually be able to be very much themselves. You thought you weren't going to be interesting enough, or funny enough.'

These feelings are very familiar to girls and women, and illustrate the way that seeking and not adequately receiving approval and encouragement from significant people such as parents can undermine the development of women's confidence in themselves, and that this can begin at a very early age. It also seems to be particularly true of male approval, and reflects the higher worth and status still given to men in society, and the inbalance in power between men and women. Men are generally less present in the home and less concerned with day-to-day activities. They are often brought in as the final arbiter or disciplinarian in some domestic issue which means that their opinion may be implicitly valued more than that of mothers.

Gill, like Fiona, also grew up in a single-parent family, but while Fiona lived with her mother after her father left, twenty-three-year-old Gill spent her early years with her father and younger brother. Although he cared for them, her father was preoccupied with working through his broken relationship with their mother. He did not have much work or money at that time and family life was very hard. He was very strict and made it clear he wanted his children to achieve well. Although she performed quite well at school, Gill cannot recall his ever giving her much encouragement or praise. She rebelled in her teens, which led to many fierce clashes between her and her father, and she eventually left home to live with a boyfriend.

Now in her early twenties and on her own with her small son Gill rarely sees her father, who has remarried and started a new family and is doing reasonably well in the photographic work he took up some years previously. She feels resentful and bitter; she has little self-confidence and is still looking for the approval she feels her father never gave her:

'I had to be a hundred per cent all the time and I got nothing in return. And in the end I couldn't see the point of it, working my butt off for what – to be criticised. I used to get migraine head-aches and totally depressed at school. It got worse and worse and it was because my dad was putting so much pressure on me, and he got disappointed in what I should've been. . . . He used to think the worst things about me so I always saw the worst things about myself. . . . My father is the only person in this world who

can affect me by passing judgement on me and this is why I've got
the lousiest view in the world of myself because he has convinced
me that I'm a terrible human being, by the way he reacts. He
doesn't realise how much recognition I need from him, what it
means to me. If I do something, a hundred people could say it's
really good but if my dad comes in and looks down his nose . . .'

Gill's father has little idea that he affects his daughter in this
way, he finds her conflictive to deal with and prefers instead to
concentrate on his second wife and baby daughter, and his career.

If we have identified strongly with someone close to us, like our
father or mother, we often absorb some of their attitudes and
beliefs, even if they do not coincide with our own, and censure
ourselves in the same way that we think they would do. They
become our internal judging mechanism, like Freud's concept of
'super-ego'. For example, Anne had an extremely close relationship with her father in the 1960s and 1970s when she was young
and has taken on many of his beliefs. It was always her and him
together, excluding her mother, and they developed a high level
of emotional interdependence which has continued into Anne's
adult life. He is now retired from the fire service and she works
in advocacy. Some of his beliefs conflict with her own views, and
she is well aware if they do because this divergence can be quite
painful for her and hard to ignore:

'I always know when I haven't worked something out in my mind
because I think "Oh, my dad won't like this" even now. Although
if I'm clear about it then I don't care what he says. Once when I
went to live with someone I knew he'd hate it because I wasn't
married. But when I knew I definitely wanted to do it, that was
all right, but I went through a phase of "Oh, dad won't like it."
I'm still very affected by thinking what he will think. It's changing,
but he's been tremendously powerful, and I worry about him
disapproving . . . like I now also realise there's this tremendous
political divergence between he and I, and that's painful.'

As we reach adulthood our relationships with our parents
usually become more equal. However, these kinds of relationships, like any other long-term close relationship, have established
patterns which cannot be easily altered, and the presence or
absence of approval can contribute significantly to the nature of
these. Kate and her father provide an illustration of this. She is
twenty-eight and working as a secretary. When she was young her

father ran a small shop with her mother. He has been a very dominant figure in her life and a person who, like many men, finds it hard to express his feelings, emotions or vulnerabilities. When she was growing up, Kate was hurt and confused when her father apparently withdrew from her in her teens, leaving her feeling very rejected by this and his obvious denial of her sexuality. (She also describes her experience in Chapter 4, which explores aspects of sexuality.) From this time, her father gave her no praise or encouragement, yet she still loves him deeply and does everything she can to be the daughter she thinks will make him really happy. She writes:

'Even as a grown woman of twenty-eight I find myself moderating myself and trying really hard to be a person he can be proud of. I notice a change in myself when I'm near dad and a strong need to show him what I can do, have achieved or aspire to. I know through therapy that I feel a deep loss because he wasn't able to tell me he was proud of me or that he loved me. . . . Another way dad affected me is in the way I make decisions. I often try to please everyone so I deny what I need . . . I think this is to do with his not acknowledging my achievements and me wanting so much to please him . . . I mask my relationship with my long-term live-in boyfriend so as not to make my dad feel less important and yet my dad, although much better, still can't be as close as I sincerely feel he would like.'

This is an aspect of the father–daughter relationship also revealed in Judith Arcana's work in which she observes how fathers' behaviour, such as being absent, having little to do with their daughters' upbringing, showing little or no affection, and being violent, can still result in their daughters loving them and seeking their affection and approval. She suggests that women excuse their fathers in a way that they would never excuse their mothers.[2]

Lack of adequate love or approval from someone as important in your development as your father can clearly have long-term effects on this relationship, and this has also been Bridget's experience. Bridget, now aged sixty-three, the youngest of two sisters, wrote describing the intensity of her relationship with her father, a white-collar worker in the docks, whose praise she yearned for and whose criticism she feared. When she was in her twenties she and her father had a major row, after which she stormed out of the family home. Although they made it up, for a long time she didn't feel that she wanted to be close to him and due to his sudden death when she was thirty she was never able to repair their relationship. Here she looks back on how he influencd her as a child:

'I was a very adoring, even a worshipping little girl. My father was a dominant and often attractive personality, who craved attention, admiration and respect. I gave him all that but never felt I got much back in return. In consequence I had low self-esteem. The times I had his attention are still highlights in my memory. . . . Life revolved around my father and his wishes and needs when we were all at home. My father was proud of me as I was a clever little girl – a bookworm as they used to call me – but I had difficulty with arithmetic and dreaded his criticism, he was good with figures. Having written this down I see how much he meant to me and remember how I never felt I could please him. The memory is still quite painful. My father was a staunch Tory, a snob and a racist. I hate having to say his, but it's important. I believed every word my father said up to the age of twenty-two which is when I began to change and was influenced by others. . . . When I could vote, at twenty-one, I voted Tory of course! And was so pleased to please my father. He clearly was a very important, perhaps the most important influence in my childhood. I was very close to and admired my mother, but I didn't look up to her in the same way. (I should have!) He was always right as far as I was concerned.'

Once again, it is the dominance and power attributed to fathers that sustains the hold that they can exert over their children of both sexes.

If many women have such a strong need for their fathers (or men in any other significant role) to genuinely praise what they are doing, it is tragic that so many men cannot adequately express their feelings and their love and approval. Contributing to this is the nature of boys' early upbringing, the role models that they grow up identifying with and conforming to, and their lack of practice in articulating a language of emotions and feelings. Traditional masculine culture has allowed little space for the exposure of feelings. This implies vulnerability, which may under-mine male power on the assumption that it is in contradiction with exerting authority. No wonder that so many women grow up feeling they are always trying to prove something to a father who will not or cannot acknowledge it or reciprocate with appropriate encouragement. He is apparently unpleasable. This emotional inbalance is also characteristic in the ways men and women communicate in a variety of situations, both public and private, as Deborah Tannen has illustrated.[3] It is women who put the most emotional input into relationships with men, whether it be with their fathers or lovers.

A need for approval can begin early in life, as illustrated by the behaviour Patrick has noticed in his four-year-old daughter Ella. Being students, he and Ella's mother Josie have both been able to participate in looking after their daughter, but he notices that Ella sometimes behaves differently with him than with Josie:

'She tends to misbehave less with me as though she is trying harder to please me and win my approval, even though I don't expect any more of her than I think Josie does. Indeed I am told that she idolizes me, in her nursery teacher's words, not that I myself realised this . . . maybe the fact that other people are telling me points to a lack of awareness or total appreciation of the affection Ella has for me, or maybe girls are just more affectionate than boys. I do tend to spoil her, although it is obvious I do not need to win her affection. It might be that there is a lack of communication on my part, men don't always communicate their feelings very well.'

Failure to communicate feelings, and withholding praise and approval can clearly create some level of dependency in daughter–father relationships and help to perpetuate sexual inequalities and the power that men may, however unwittingly, hold over women.

If fathers tend to be unforthcoming with praise or approval for their daughters, will they also do the same with their sons? Probably the answer is yes, but if so, it may also be that sons do not rely so much on this for their positive psychological development. It is more likely, however, that they do and that the negative effects may be similar, but these are repressed or transformed into an outward show of masculine characteristics which disguise lack of confidence and self-esteem. A son may feel the same need or desire for approval but be less willing to recognise or express it. Wanting but not receiving enough approval from their fathers, they may also identify so strongly with them that in some ways they take on the identity of their fathers and can thereby, unlike girls in this position, achieve some level of independence from them. They may also find it harder than women to admit, or be more able to ignore their desire for their father's approval.

It is also necessary to look at the question of mothers' approval. Although there are both boys and girls who are anxious to prove themselves in some particular way to their mother, it is not generally as unforthcoming or problematic as paternal approval. Where mothers are nurturant and caring, their love and approval is assumed as a basic part of the relationship, whereas for fathers and children this is not so. The greater psychological distance between them, as well as the higher status still often associated with men inside and outside the home, means that men are set up as the more important judges of behaviour and personality, and are deemed harder or more important to please.

While I have so far illustrated the potential and the consequences of girls' general desire to please, it is often specifically in approval for achievements – whether at school, college or work – that fathers often play an important role. While mothers may also be significant, for those daughters describing their experiences here they are mentioned much less in this context. Their love and approval, although important, is usually made less conditional on this kind of performance. A lot of these women emphasised how important their father's aspirations and expectations were to them; as well as interest or participation in their school life, positive attitudes towards their education, and the ability to award praise or encouragement in whatever they were doing. Research done in the area of achievement motivation has suggested that high-achieving girls have often had a close relationship with their fathers and have identified with them.[4] Some of this original work was done many years ago in families in which men and women took more traditional roles. It would be interesting to explore whether there were any such effects on daughters in families where mothers held high-level, powerful jobs.

It is natural for parents to be proud of their children's achievements, and to say so. Many do, but some fail to express this adequately or at all. Some parents even believe that praising children will make them complacent and lazy and they will stop working so well. Tony, whose fifteen-year-old daughter Laura was quoted earlier in the chapter, is such a parent. He has a managerial job with the electricity board and lives with his wife, eighteen-year-old son Martin, and Laura. Although he is very pleased with

Laura's school performance she has to find this out secondhand, as she describes:

'I think he has a bit more respect for me now, but I don't know how much. It doesn't show that often, only when he's introducing me to people, like on New Year's Eve this bloke said "Your dad's really proud of you." I thought "Wow, I didn't know that." I suppose it's intelligence more than anything else I've done. I took my maths a year early and when I did well in it he said "Well done" and left it at that. All my other relatives went "Oh brilliant! Really good." My dad plays low-key. When I got my certificate he said "Good, just what I thought". But apparently he was really proud of me. I think I'd like him to say it to me. It would make me feel better in myself knowing that it's appreciated.'

Tony takes the view that he has to adopt a less enthusiastic attitude for Laura to continue achieving well:

'From her being about three years old, I've not had worries about Laura. She's got grit, determination, she takes opportunities. You don't worry about somebody like that. You encourage, play it down, that's a way of encouraging it. She sailed through primary school. On effort she got straight 'A's on every subject and on ability as well. She brought the report to me and I sat and read it with a very sombre face. I said "Well kid, we'll treasure that. That's excellent. There isn't a chance that you can repeat this, but we'll treasure that one." So that gave the encouragement. The challenge went down . . . I don't over-praise her and that's probably hard. Under-praising is as hard as over-praising. I believe that the under-praising actually keeps the steel there with Laura. Too much credit leaves her nothing to try for, so it is made light of. But I'm sure that she knows that it in no way demeans her or what she has achieved. She's very balanced and rounded, very mature. I'm lucky with her. She has tremendous ability and I would hate to see that wasted. I'd be a little disappointed if she went into marriage and kids. I dearly want her to produce grandchildren, I want her to be fulfilled, but I do want her to do what she's capable of.'

Tony thinks he is challenging Laura by under-praising her, which she is aware of, but is rather disappointed by. However, he has also unintentionally issued a stronger challenge when he recently told the family how he identified with his son when he was born, which he describes in Chapter 1. Laura remembers how she reacted:

'On my brother's eighteenth birthday dad told us he'd felt ecstatic when he was born, he felt a union with him, "Wow, my son!" and said he hadn't felt like that after that. I said "Not when I was born?" "Well no, you were different, you were a girl. I didn't know what it was like to be a girl." That hit me, I didn't like it. It made me want to prove myself more. I really studied. I'm going to work like mad for the rest of my GCSEs to prove I can do it. It did hurt when he said that, but then I thought it through and thought, well he didn't actually treat me any differently when I was smaller. I think he's made the best of it. . . . He makes me want to prove things I suppose, because I'm a girl really. He's a bit sexist – "The woman's place is in the home" – up to a point. I think he wants me to get what I can. He doesn't say "Get married, have kids, stay at home". But I've got to prove myself that I can do that, the career, more than anything really, whereas Martin hasn't got to prove himself, because dad kind of expects that of him anyway, so in some ways it's slightly harder for me.'

If challenging by under-praising has worked in some measure for Laura, it may not do so for others who may be demoralised and try less hard as a result. It depends on many factors such as individual personality, level of self-esteem, and the nature of the father–daughter relationship. For example, Maria comes from a Greek-Cypriot family. She is nineteen and soon to be married to her Greek-Cypriot boyfriend. Throughout her teenage years, she consistently rebelled against her father's over-protection and his attempts to restrict her social activities. It is customary for Cypriot families to be strict in monitoring girls' social and sexual activities, so as not to tarnish the family reputation or reduce the chances of a good marriage. Maria and her father are obviously fond of each other and he is very generous to her in lots of ways, but he has shown little confidence in her abilities and she has received no encouragement from him as far as things like school and work are concerned. Like Laura, she perceives this as his way of challenging her and fortunately has developed enough self-determination to take on his negative attitudes as something else to resist and rebel against:

'He's always saying "Oh, you'll never do that." He wants to push me to do better so he thinks if he says that, I'll try and prove him wrong, and I do try my best. But he's never encouraged me, never. It was the same with my driving test. I failed the first test. When I came home after the second one and I'd passed, he just said "Oh, well done." I was so happy that day, everyone was, but he didn't even hardly acknowledge it. I was very disappointed. The same with my exams. He never thought I'd do it, and with getting a job, he said "You'll never get anything". He doesn't say it now because I've proved him wrong. And like getting engaged and getting married, that's another thing added to it. He never thought I'd do it, but I am, although I don't think I'd ever do anything like that unless I wanted to do it.'

The nature of the father–daughter relationships during childhood, and through the often stormy adolescent years when children are trying to develop an independent sense of self-identity, is very important in determining the direction in which this relationship moves. For example, Meena is another daughter who reacted against the restrictiveness of her father when she was young. She is now thirty-two and lives in the south of England with her husband and two small daughters. Her father was a painter and art teacher who died when she was twenty-five. He was from Pakistan and her mother is English. She grew up like an only child because her younger sister was not born until she was twenty-two. There was a lot of conflict between her and her father during her adolescence, exacerbated by her father's religion and cultural background. Although he was not a practising Muslim, as she herself observed: 'Old habits die hard'. She always felt her parents were very critical and took her achievements for granted. Although she went to a girls' grammar school and then took history at university, she had been trying to rebel against her family and cultural background even before reaching her teens. She wanted to fail the 11+ exam (but passed it), and aspired to marry early and have four children. She comments:

'This was in reaction to my parents, my father particularly, who thought it was really easy for me to be a creative person. [He thought] of course I could write if I wanted to, after all, he'd earned his pocket money as a boy by doing so and being published in newspapers. I wonder now if I've under-achieved because of this attitude. I didn't write, paint etc. because it was expected that I would. So I bloodymindedly wanted to do something else. I've achieved my "get married" ideal to a certain extent, and all the boyfriends I've ever had have been from "working-class" back-grounds, very unpretentious, not particularly ambitious, although the serious relationships have been with "clever" ones. My husband is the apotheosis of these – a Yorkshireman who is quiet, shy and a teetotaller.'

Although Meena's father professed many liberal-minded ideas about issues such as sex before marriage, men and women living together, foreign travel for women and homosexuality, Meena discovered that these freedoms were not meant to apply to herself. She found this contradiction very confusing, but chose to pursue several of them anyway. Her father had an aggressive relationship with her and her mother which eventually made it very difficult for Meena to love and respect him:

'When I was growing up I thought he was handsome and I was somehow proud of him, but he was so lousy with people and treated them so badly. . . . I thought [my mother] sacrificed everything of herself to him. When he went into a rage she just went quiet. I wanted her to rage back and tell him how stupid he was. I thought he emotionally battered her. He could pour on the scorn and hatred with words, but mostly with his eyes. I shouted back and argued and cried. . . . My mother said "I love him". I didn't think this was good enough. For years and years I wanted them to divorce. I didn't have any reconciliations with my father, we just had continual battles about everything. In between silences, we didn't talk about anything. We avoided being in the same room together. We had nothing to talk about. I talked about everything with my mother in the kitchen. . . . I felt he hated me, scorned me, was against me in everything, and completely failed to communicate with me. Nothing I ever did was good enough but apparently when I wasn't there he spoke of me proudly, and spoke in fact largely of me. Can I believe it?'

Meena could never reconcile herself with her father's attitudes and his treatment of herself and her mother, and their relationship could never be retrieved. She experienced little sense of love and encouragement from her father, however proud he may have appeared to outsiders. Meena was not alone in having a father who spoke proudly or boastfully about her to others, while not telling her himself. Characteristics of the father–daughter relation-ship like withholding encouragement and approval cut across social background, affecting both middle class and working class, although this may arise from a variety of historical precedents. Sheila, for example, who now lives in Wales, had a very different upbringing from her father, who had been brought up in Ireland with no formal education. At seventeen he came to the north of England where he married Sheila's mother, and Sheila was the first of their five children. Her father was very violent and Sheila had a miserable and disturbed childhood (which she describes in Chapter 3). The direction of her life altered dramatically in her teens. She writes:

'After years of under-achievement at school a lovely teacher suggested I might be university material. From then [aged about thirteen] that was my goal. My schoolwork became all-important and I was totally single-minded about it. It was hard because I had nowhere to study at home and the atmosphere was not conducive to study. Also, with both parents in full-time employment, a lot of domestic responsibilities fell on me. I think my father was proud of how well I was doing at school. He told his friends at work that I was set for college, that I'd passed nine O-levels in one go. He never told me. In fact, he was on at me to do the housework, complained that I always had my nose in a book and sneered at how unattractive, awkward and generally horrible I was. I think he was afraid of me.'

These kinds of male fears and insecurities often find expression within the family, where a man's relative position of physical or economic power means he can potentially dominate his wife or children. This position is complicated further if he feels threatened by a daughter who is more intelligent and/or attaining a higher or more 'academic' status as teacher, student, etc. than himself. In Sheila's case this was probably further accentuated by her mother's attainments: she had gained a grammar school scholarship and trained as a secretary and therefore also had a higher level of education than her husband.

A similar situation existed within Olwen's family, where her father was also threatened by the achievements of his wife and daughter. Olwen's childhood in Wales with her parents in the 1960s was characterised by long periods when her father was away from home in the navy, followed by periods of unemployment when he finished his service. She had consequently developed a closer relationship with her mother, who worked as a teacher. Now aged thirty-seven, she recalls her father's attitude and behaviour when she went to university:

'Sometimes my father would not even allow me and my mother to have a conversation in the same room as him, especially after I went to college: anything I said to her was interpreted as the two of us deliberately excluding him, ganging up even; I had so much I wanted to express about my experience as a student in Oxford but I could not even mention the name of the place if he was present because he would explode. Yet he would always boast to his friends that his daughter was at Oxford.'

It is sad that such insecurity and the need to present an external image of success means that a daughter like Olwen may decorate her father's ego outside the home, but has to be put in her place within it.

Another example of this kind of male insecurity is illustrated by Lisa's family. She is an only child, now aged thirty, whose father was a skilled manual worker. She describes him as 'semi-literate' and 'working class to the core' while her mother, a miner's daughter, had worked as a teacher and eventually become a headmistress. There was always a lot of conflict between Lisa and her father. Lisa thought he had always seen her as a problem and when she went to school and it became apparent she was quite bright, this seemed to widen the gap between them. She writes:

'In company dad would boast of my intelligence, as if my ability were somehow compensating for his lack. This again embarrassed me. I did not wish to be made to look more different than I already was. For all his boasting dad never attended parents' evenings or had any direct dealings with the school beyond going to the Carol Concert. All that was mum's department. Long before I could put my feelings into words, I knew that I was a prop for his ego, something to add to his stature in society – but not a person in my own right. He would play boisterous games with me when visitors called, games we didn't play when they weren't there, then people left thinking what a good father he was. I knew his boasting about my schoolwork was based on secondhand information for he knew next to nothing about how a primary school operated. . . . My intelligence was probably a threat and I had to be reminded of who was the boss. (Who was he kidding! Any fool could see mum was the dominant one in our house.)'

The reaction of Lisa's father to her educational achievements was to use them to enhance his own self-image while not giving her much encouragement or support nor any involvement in her school activities. It is interesting that these three examples that arose in the research are all families in which there are no sons with whom the father could identify, and their daughters were more intelligent than their fathers or had taken up better opportunities. The daughters are also from working-class backgrounds but they have moved out of these through gaining higher education. It is also relevant to consider the historical period in which some of these women were growing up. This was the 1950s and 1960s, following the Second World War. There is something specific to this generation of postwar children, some of whom reaped the benefits of the 1944 Education Act which implemented a three-tier educational system. Passing or failing the 11+ exam propelled these children into either grammar school, secondary modern school or technical college. Each of these had its appropriate levels of achievement and expected positions in the labour force. Unlike the earlier part of the century, the prevailing ideology at this time emphasised equal education for all, regardless of sex or class. However, the grammar schools inevitably tended to be filled predominately by middle-class children, while secondary moderns and technical colleges mainly accomodated children from working-class backgrounds.

This system did, nevertheless, provide an opportunity that many parents were determined to seize for their children. For girls in particular, a place at grammar school provided the chance to pursue a good job or career, an aim that contradicted the current ideology of the family, which still saw their essential role as wives and mothers at home. Many achieved O-levels and A-levels and went into higher education; others left earlier but often returned to education years later as mature students. Many of the latter had experienced the conflicts of trying to combine women's double role of family and work, and identified with the feminist ideas expressed within the women's movement at that time. Many of those who contacted me about their father–daughter relationships were in their late thirties and forties and shared common aspects of this history, as I do myself.

Elaine also comes from this generation, but unlike the examples quoted earlier, her working-class father was very encouraging and supportive to her and her two sisters pursuing education and careers. Now aged forty-four, she grew up in a country village and went to the local grammar school. She rebelled at school and left at fifteen to take a secretarial course, eventually leaving home to take up a job in London. Later she emigrated to work in Canada for seven years before returning to England to go to art school and become a ceramic potter. She comes from a working-class family, the eldest of three sisters. Her father Jim originally started working on the railways as a 'greaser boy' and ended up running the ticket office in the village where they lived. He had once taken a scholarship but not passed it, and her mother had gained two scholarships but could not take them up because her family had financial problems. In keeping with the traditional ideology of women's place in the family, Elaine's father did not want her mother to go out to work and she never did so. However, as Elaine describes, unlike her mother's experience, they were both very keen that Elaine and her sisters pursue the advantages of education and careers:

'My father thought it was more important to concentrate more on things that would enable us to earn our own living than on more feminine things. If there were any spare resources they went into our education instead of the house. This is tied in with the time I was born, and passing the 11+, me being bright and there being grammar schools and opportunities for people of my generation. It's tied in with the missed opportunities of my parents . . . and with it being postwar and us being working-class kids.'

Jim was not threatened by his daughters' attaining greater knowledge than himself. He was pleased for them and it did not bother him that their 'power' of knowledge had become greater than his own. For her reaction, Elaine remembers how, when he visited her in London, her higher level of education and sophistication made her feel responsible and protective:

'I felt this is my dad from the country in the big city, I think it was to do with knowledge. Then at one point in my life I knew I was earning more than my father and that was a slight embarrassment; and having a working-class father or a bit of a country bumpkin and there I was in the big city holding my own. But now I realise that with the background my father came from – his father was a shepherd – he'd done quite well.'

Rosemary, whose father–daughter relationship has been described in Chapter 1, is another daughter from this same generation. Her father had been an insurance salesman, and he had high aspirations for her. In childhood they had a turbulent relationship, and when she did fulfil his academic hopes it presented him with a potentially conflicting prospect, as Rosemary explains:

'I think he always assumed that I was intelligent and bright. I remember he taught me how to spell things and how to read dictionaries. Then I ended up going to grammar school and knowing more than him, I think that added yet another dimension to the whole thing because I had a bit more power. He always expected a lot of me. He was delighted when I passed my 11+ exam, promised me a pony that I didn't get. He was pleased about university, but he was also anxious because the pill had become freely available two years before. The whole issue about me and sexuality and my dad is a fraught one, so his delight and pleasure was tainted by knowing that there was no way I was going to stay a virgin. He wouldn't have thought about it in these terms but he certainly was worried about me.'

This level of conflict between paternal protection and achievement aspirations is less common nowadays, but still exists and is also the norm in families with cultural backgrounds which specify that girls should remain virtually or totally sexually inexperienced until marriage.

Another example of fathers who expect much from their daughters is provided by John, a seventy-year-old who has always been overly aware of being deprived of the opportunity to pursue education in his childhood. John is pleased that his four daughters all entered careers like teaching or nursing. He was forced to leave school at a young age to be channelled into the family business, which he hated and later abandoned to take on a new career in farming. After an unhappy childhood, and harbouring deep regret for his lack of education, his main concern in life has been his aspirations for his children. They are a close family and, as the only male figure, John's strong views and critical nature have had a powerful and almost oppressive effect on his daughters. The youngest, Barbara, aged twenty-eight, took a teaching degree, got married and later left teaching to have her daughter, now aged two. She describes her father's attitudes:

'If you've got your parents influencing you too strongly you can't ever escape. He had very strong views about careers and I think that influenced me with my career. He wanted us to do a career that he considered useful, like nursing or teaching . . . I think he would have been happy if one of us had said we want to take the

farm over, but none of us were anywhere near doing that. I think
he would have liked me to marry a farmer. . . . To him the family's
the most important thing. He's proud of what we've done. At least
we've done what he wanted us to do, become teachers and nurses
and then settled down and had families! I think he's quite happy,
although he might say something different!'

John did in fact say something a little different, and although it
was clear that essentially he was very pleased with what they had
achieved, what he had really wanted them to do was to get degrees:

'The all-important thing for me was to get them through higher
education, it was important for them to have a career. It hasn't
been easy but we've managed, they've all qualified. I'm pleased,
I can't be proud because realistically it's not a terribly great
achievement but I'm delighted about it. They're just not academic:
teaching and nursing are not on a par with a degree in English or
philosophy, but the careers themselves are very, very good. I had
something of the feeling that they had to do it to satisfy me but
there was never any question that they wouldn't do it. I'm only
disappointed that it isn't enough: Barbara's the only one that went
to university and that's the level of education I wanted for them.
. . . I feel so strongly that what you do to your children from
nought to twelve you can't get rid of. I resent bitterly my lack of
education and I suppose that's why.'

As well as pressurising his daughters to achieve well, John has
also tried to compensate for his own lack of education by success-
fully taking up painting and taking a number of academic courses
at home. He is a strong character and now in old age, his daughters
often find themselves colluding to please and protect him from
anything that might provoke hurt or disapproval.

Young people's achievements in relation to their parents are
obviously not only dependent on their determination and abilities,
and the parental encouragement and approval they receive, although
these all play their part. They are also influenced by the historical
interplay of the economy, education policies and the state of the
job market. Many children growing up in the 1980s and 1990s have
been faced with youth training or income support instead of jobs
and careers, and student loans to put them into early debt at
college or university. They have very different choices from the
optimistic postwar generation and may be more destined to
disappoint the hopes of their parents than exceeding them.

Many fathers, like John and Jim quoted here, hope that their children will achieve many of the things that they never had the opportunities to take up. Those who have succeeded in achieving these goals for themselves hope that their children will do the same. Richard had changed his career and status by leaving his work as technical representative and going to university as a mature student to study history, which he really enjoyed. When his daughter Sophie got a place in a small, provincial university and revealed that she wanted to go into teaching, it wasn't quite what Richard had in mind:

'I think for the most part one projects one's own unfulfilled ambitions on to one's children, although in a sense mine were fulfilled, if rather late. In life you get everything you want but not necessarily when you want. I lived my life backwards. To be realistic I would like her to know things, to me the point of education is enlightenment, I want to know about things. If she wants to teach that's fine, but on the other hand if she's capable of going further then I'd like her to, but in the end you come down to her. I was distinctly disappointed that history wasn't her interest. I don't harp on to her though.'

Sophie appreciates that her father respects her choice and has not seriously tried to persuade her any differently, and she has the confidence to pursue what she wants to do:

'I think he was a bit disappointed. I really want to teach and I think he thinks I could do something more academic. All the same he never tries to push me, he's never said "You should do this", it's more like "Don't you think you'll get bored?" I wouldn't want him to be telling me what to do because then I know I wouldn't do it. I'd think he had less respect for my point of view then. He might not agree with it but he feels it's up to me. I would be upset if I thought he was trying to make up my mind for me and that he didn't trust me to make it up myself. My mum's the same. She didn't go to university or anything. She doesn't think "I wish she'd done history" like my dad does. I think she's just very pleased and I think in a way she hasn't got such high ideals for me as my dad has, she can see that maybe I'll be happy teaching. I think she feels, let her get on with it, whereas perhaps my dad, I get the impression he feels he'd like to organise me but feels he shouldn't.'

Sophie is confident in what she wants, and although aware of her parents' feelings, does not feel overly pressured in any way.

There are, however, those daughters who feel the force of their successful parent's expectations for them quite acutely. In contrast to those women who represent a threat to their less educated or lower-achieving fathers, there are those who feel oppressed by their fathers' attitudes and high aspirations for them. Fiona, for instance (who early in this chapter recalled her attempts to seek the elusive approval of her journalist father, David), knew that her father would respect her more if she worked in the arts as he had done. Although she eventually trained in ceramics, which comes within his realm of artistic approval, she had previously considered some quite different options. David had seen these as inappropriate and had therefore been very discouraging. She recalls the time when she wanted to go into nursing:

'I always wanted to do something he approved of, I know if I'd gone into television or something he would have been impressed with me. Once when I was about fifteen I said I wanted to be a nurse and I remember he wrote me this letter saying "The last thing on earth you want to be is a nurse, it's just a skivvy for men doctors", and it was something I really wanted to do so it was really damning. I never did it, although I think I didn't not do it because he said that – maybe I thought it was true in some ways. But I was really hurt.'

David also remembers this occasion, and his other hopes for her:

'Fiona got very angry with me once at the time when she was doing this nursing thing. I said "It's not the way to do it. The thing to do is we'll get you into some place, be properly trained and be a doctor. Don't be a nurse. Much as we all admire nurses, it is quite a low-level job." But she was very put out at that for some reason. She seemed to think it was typically elitist of me. I didn't think there was any point in being anything unless you were at the top. Then she started making pottery and I thought that was wonderful. I wanted her, and I still want her, to be successful at that. I want her to be able to say, when people ask "Who are you?" to say "I am a potter." Then, "I am the mother of these two children", and to go on through things but to start off with what is individual, a creation she's made out of herself. . . . I believe strongly in your work, if you're lucky enough to have interesting work I think that's more important than almost anything else. Husbands and wives will come and go, children will grow up, but your work will always be there.'

Fiona had recently been helping people with disabilities which, although admirable in her father's eyes, is not the sort of 'creative' and more glamorous work that he would have preferred.

Paternal approval or disapproval can play an important role in women's achievement, the way they relate to other people, especially men, as well as in other areas of their lives. As we have seen, many factors influence the nature and depth of each individual father–daughter relationship, and the expectations embedded within it. If approval is made conditional on children doing what their parents think is best for them, as it often is, then this can clearly lead to a clash of interests and a withholding of approval. When approval takes into account children's own needs and desires, however, this can provide pride and pleasure on both sides. What is important is not only giving approval itself, but giving it for achievement on the child's own terms, which is harder to do. Margaret, for example, is emphatic on this point. As described earlier, she grew up in a Jewish family who expected and hoped that she would get a job and marry and settle down with a home and children. Her parents were not at all concerned about her doing well in further education, as her father Raymond confirms:

'We thought that she should go out to work rather than carry on an academic life. We virtually pushed her out, thinking that it would be the academic side that would set her on the downhill path and mix with the wrong sort of people. We tended to think that college was a nest of bad influence. If we got her out to work she would mix with a better set. We got her a job with the BBC initially . . . but it wasn't too long before she decided that she was going to do what job she wanted and not what we thought was best for her.'

Margaret did not conform to her parents' wishes, and although she married early and had a daughter it was not under the circumstances that her parents would have liked. Eventually the marriage broke down and some years later Margaret went back to education to fulfil her own academic aspirations, and then was delighted at the response:

'It was my father that sent me the card when I passed my Master's. Father's approval! It meant so much to me. It was so nice, the education thing, because that was like approval on my terms of what I wanted. I desperately wanted success, and it was approval of something that *I* wanted approval for, not approval of things that I hadn't wanted approval for, which it was before, and that's wonderful. He still comes down and talks about what I'm doing and he's interested. They're proud of what I'm doing. It means a lot. I think that's why I feel closer to them. I think it's really important that parents give their kids approval on the kids' terms, because you want things for kids, like they wanted things for me but I didn't want them. It's very difficult to turn round and want what your kids want.'

Raymond concurred:

'She has achieved a lot now in the educational field and I am warmly proud of her. Maybe I don't tell her as much as I should, but I am. I talk to other people, I am proud of her.'

Raymond's words now have a familiar ring. If fathers give daughters the encouragement, praise and approval that they usually desire and deserve, this can have significant effects on their relationship with their daughter as well as her subsequent achievements.

This chapter has been devoted to illustrating aspects of father–daughter approval and achievement because this cropped up so frequently in interviews and letters. As with many other factors in the father–daughter relationship, the patterns are varied. For instance, research has suggested that high-achieving daughters have often had a close and supportive relationship with their fathers. While I agree with this, I would also suggest that some daughters have achieved well in spite of their fathers. There are many interacting factors in this, not least of which is the nature of the mother–daughter relationship which, in terms of the increased education and career achievements attained by many women, may now be quite different from two or three decades ago, when achievement motivation was a more fashionable topic for study. Although I have concentrated here on approval in the context of achievements and the consequent way daughters view themselves, paternal approval can have implications for other areas of girls' lives. For example, a father can also be important in the development of his daughter's sexual identity and confidence by means of his recognition and approval of her as a sexual and attractive person, as is explored in Chapter 4. If daughters value such parental approval, this can also have powerful and positive effects on their levels of self-esteem and self-confidence. While it should be easy for fathers (like some of those described here) to do this, many are unreasonably reticent in directly expressing this to their daughters.

Chapter 3

Dominance and violence

'None of us has ever had a stand–up argument with him. We'll argue, and he shouts, and you stand and listen. You don't answer back, it's not a two–way thing. You just sit and take it, because he's my father. My dad never hit any of us, but he never needed to. He just had to say "Don't do that" and you did what he said. You didn't want to upset him, nobody did.'

Jean

'He'd say, "I know you're telling lies, I can see it in your eyes." My dad and God – I wasn't sure of the difference between the two of them at all. I always used to think it would have been nice to have been a Catholic so I could have gone to confession.'

Rosemary

'It wasn't just that he was violent in that he would beat you up or hit you, he is also the most totally dominating, all–possessing man. You're not allowed to have any opinion at all, everything has to be under his shadow, he has to control everything, what you eat, what you wear, where you go.'

Judy

The traditional role of the father is a dominant and powerful one. It has its roots in a patriarchal system that places men as fathers at the head of the family as well as many other social institutions. Even though in Britain today we no longer endorse such strict values and attitudes, they are by no means extinct. They are present in people's assumptions about value differences in sex roles and between feminine and masculine personalities. Many children are familiar with threats like 'Wait until your father comes home', implying the patriarchal characteristics of authority, strength and punishment. The male role is linked with physical and sexual violence, and domination. Obviously, most men do not demonstrate these attributes to excess but there are a significant number who do; and the fact that men still dominate the social, economic and political structure, and often wield unequal power and authority within their families, clearly demonstrates that authority is still predominately divided according to sex.

Women generally hold the family together in terms of daily organisation and, as part of this, it is common for them to take responsibility for maintaining authority in routine domestic matters. Fathers also play their part in this, but they are often appealed to as a stronger authority or as an external arbitor. Thus in many girls' lives, mother is the soft option on discipline compared to father. For example, this was the case in Laura's family (quoted in earlier chapters). She lives with her parents and older brother in the northwest of England. Fifteen-year-old Laura confirms this sexual division of authority at home:

'I suppose my dad is the one we were more frightened of if we'd done anything wrong, and we'd say to mum "Don't tell dad". Mum will yell, but it doesn't make the same impact. I don't think my dad would hit me or anything like that, he'd just really shout at me, and I get wound up and shout back, I suppose because I'm like him.' On this subject, her father commented:

'There have been times when I've laid the law down and said "No", but I don't regard that as a clash. She may think sometimes I'm very serious, but when I say it I mean it. They have to know when you mean it, otherwise it doesn't mean anything. I suppose they could see it as dogmatic, but I don't really try to look at myself through their eyes.'

For some children, and probably daughters in particular, the psychological effects of parents' anger can be sufficient castigation. For example, Richard, (who has previously described bringing up his nineteen-year-old daughter Sophie in the West Country) spoke of his daughter's childhood reactions to discipline:

'The truth was, it was never necessary to smack her. If one raised one's voice, she would dissolve into tears, so one had to be very careful, even speaking sharply to her.'

Sophie confirmed this:

'I can remember with my dad, he only had to look at me, it would really upset me. But I think they both used to tell me off, my mum a bit more, maybe because she was around more. But more than tell me off, they used to sort of explain to me – "You shouldn't do that because . . ."'.

In Sophie's family, things are openly explained and discussed and physical punishment is out of the question but other parents may take a different view. There are many families in which a slap is seen as being the most appropriate response to misbehaviour. There are many children too, who prefer a quick slap as punishment instead of hours of talking or some kind of psychological punishment, such as ostracism or a withdrawal of treats or privileges. It is sometimes thought that methods of family discipline vary by class in that the middle class are stereotyped as spending time painstakingly explaining their child's misdemeanours so she or he will not do it again, while working-class parents prefer to give her or him a clip round the ear. To whatever extent that this may be true, it is more a reflection of the differences in economic and social conditions in working-class and middle-class homes than inherent differences in ideas about childrearing.[1] In so far as there are differences in the ways that families tend to discipline girls and boys, parents may give boys more physical punishment while girls may experience a withdrawal of parental love and affection. (Some researchers have suggested that fathers do this more than mothers.[2]) This kind of psychological discipline can cover many sorts of things, such as being ignored for a long period of time; withholding hugs and cuddles; no bedtime stories; special treats cancelled; and other important signs of love or special activities suspended as a punishment for bad behaviour which, when effective, may increase children's need for approval and their dependency.

In a two-parent family, each parent has recourse to appeal to the support or stronger discipline of the other parent. With a one-parent family, the relationship between parent and child is more intense with respect to authority because there is no other adult to be called on. Peter is a single father who in earlier chapters has described his relationship with his fourteen-year-old daughter, who alternates her weeks between him and her mother. As in many one-parent families, there is a tendency for relationships to be somewhat more equalised at a one-to-one level, especially when the children reach a more mature age. Peter comments:

'We have scraps. Sometimes it's her fault and sometimes it's mine. If she's tired or been up late or been harrassed than she'll just get really nasty, and sometimes I take out my tiredness and frustration with life and God knows what else on her. It reminds me of relationships you have with adults rather than your own offspring. I have to be quite aware of that I think, that I'm not taking stuff out on her. I've never hit her. I don't think I was ever hit as a child, so it's not in my make-up to do that. I think it probably helps the adult to get whatever's in their system out but I don't think it's any good for the kid. So if you don't do that you have to be a bit more subtle or devious about how you bend their will to link in with yours. I suppose these days I do it by glaring. You get a close-to-the-line sort of glare – "Don't do it", so there's a veiled threat I suppose. But she knows it's not really a threat, it would just be a nasty scene . . . I think that's how our discipline works. She's nearly fifteen, what threats can you make? She's got a front door key, she may never come home again.'

Whatever kind of discipline or punishment is invoked, when children are small the physical and psychological inequality of power between parent and child is unquestionable. When children get larger and stronger, especially boys, it is possible for them to physically resist the control and authority of their parents more effectively. The normal balance of control between parents and children, however, depends a lot on the implicit nature of the relationship. As children you are expected to obey your parents because they are your parents, and you should do as you are told. This is complicated by whatever feelings of love and affection exist between you and your parents, which make disobeying them a more guilt-provoking course to take. It is also affected by the desire for approval and the wish to please parents, explored in the last chapter, which in adolescence may clash head-on with rebellion and the search for independent identity. The role of fathers in all this depends on how parental authority is divided up within individual families, but they are often treated as ultimate authority figures who get drawn in when the going gets rough. Men do not necessarily want to take on this kind of role, but if they are the ones who work away from home they are sometimes called upon by mothers to act as the external judge and executor of punishment. This reinforces this dimension of patriarchal power and the inequality of power between father, mother and children. The father–daughter relationship contains two aspects of the control that men exert over women: that over the daughter as a child, and as a female. If paternal discipline and authority is exaggerated, as it clearly was in some of the families of daughters who contacted me, it may become an over-riding feature of family life and relationships and thereby exert a radical effect on girls' psychological development, their behaviour at home and at school and their views and interactions with men in general.

A significant number of women wrote or talked to me about the dominant or violent nature of their relationships with their fathers, and the rest of this chapter describes and examines some of their experiences. The all-pervasive power that a dominating father can wield over his entire family is great. It does not have to involve physical force; it can be equally effective without. An example is Eve who is forty-six and married with two children, and her father died a few years before. He always exerted a controlling influence on her and the whole family:

'My relationship with my father was not a happy one, he was an extremely domineering and overpowering person (rather like living with a volcano and waiting for it to erupt), although he never used physical violence. Somehow he seemed to control my mother, brother and myself and other family members just by some underlying power he seemed to possess, which would not be tolerated by most people and which I would never tolerate from anyone else. To outsiders, particularly in the pub, he was the life and soul of the party, but at home he was the complete opposite, and I can only say that from about the age of fourteen I came to realise that this person was making his family very unhappy and indeed the situation deteriorated to such an extent that I cannot really remember ever feeling any love towards him. Eventually, towards the end of his life I felt a certain pity but could never feel the love I felt should exist between a father and daughter.'

All relationships within the family are crucially shaped by the distribution and manifestation of power. As time goes by, the initially unequal power relations between parents and children usually change, as children mature physically and mentally and become adults themselves. But the nature of the power embedded within parent–child relationships is very strong and may endure throughout adulthood. Stella, for instance, had a very judgemental and controlling father, who was away in the army for much of her early life. He discriminated against her in favour of both her sister and her twin brother, yet she still loved him, wanted to please him, and turned him into the 'good' parent. She has been married and divorced three times, and believes her relationship with her father has made a crucial contribution to the path of her life and her other relationships, and is still doing so. She wrote of her father:

'He is still alive, eighty-two, and at Christmas was able to reduce me, a forty-nine-year old woman, to tears. I retreated to my bedroom and he is unaware of any offence.'

Such power need have nothing to do with physical threat or violence, the effects of rejection and the withdrawal of love and affection can be just as effective. David and Fiona have a father–daughter relationship that has already been described with respect to Fiona's desire for his approval. Her father is now in his sixties but he still exerts a strong psychological influence, as she describes:

'He's very charming but he is quite powerful, and I think as a child he was very powerful for me. He could really make me cringe, and he never slapped us. It was just by some little phrase, I would be really hurt by it. But I never cried, I'd hold it in, which I do now . . . . It's almost like you're powerless, because he's always been the father first, and you've always been the daughter. You can't change it.'

Non-violent paternal domination was described by other women who, at the same time, shared very caring relationships with their fathers. Barbara is an illustration, the youngest (now twenty-eight) of four daughters who were brought up on a farm. Her father John, had high educational aspirations for all of them, as was mentioned in the previous chapter. She described the way her father's strong views on everything, from education to sexuality, permeated his daughters' lives. Barbara and her sisters did not resist and challenge her father's authority; they were more amenable to the word of the father, as she observes:

'He is so dominating, he emphasises what he thinks very strongly. To some extent I think my sisters have got his values and his ideas and views. My eldest sister's the most influenced by him, she sort of aspires to be exactly like him and my mother. In a way maybe he's done right to be very strong-minded because we've all ended up with the same views and we want our children to have the same views. He's had quite a powerful effect on us. . . . But it's not good to have had such a dominating influence in such a subtle way. If it had been openly dominant, then you could fight it as a straight battle. I think it takes a longer time to come to terms with it being subtle.'

This kind of domination is certainly harder to resist, because it is not so directly confrontable, and perhaps women are more susceptible to it than men. Once again it depends on the personalities and inter-relationships of the individuals concerned, and with a different cast of characters it is also possible to envisage a female–dominated family structure like Barbara's in which it is the women who have the greater say.

Parent–child relationships are complicated by feelings of love, guilt, anger and fear of rejection, on both sides. Children live in a small and concentrated world, in which it is seen as very important to be good. If they are bad they feel guilty and want to be forgiven, and parents hold the power to grant this. Rosemary and Stanley are another daughter and father whose relationship has been described in other chapters. Stanley comes from an older generation with strong moral views on discipline and sexuality. His early relationship with his daughter, was on the one hand, quite close and they shared activities together, and on the other it was frequently characterised by her passionate defiance of him and his responding physical violence. He was very dominating and Rosemary responded by misbehaving and by bullying other people. Despite her strong resistance to his domination, she was so involved with him that he was also the only one who could forgive her:

'I was terrified of him sometimes. It was his disapproving more than the hitting, afraid that I'd be banished. He had that kind of power, just to keep me there, hanging around, because I was bad and he was the only one who could forgive me almost, nobody else would want me there because I was so dreadful. I think it hurt him a great deal, but by then he was well locked into it. He doesn't want anything challenging his right to be top dog in his little castle. As soon as I had an independence in what I wanted to do that was in any way different to what he wanted me to do, he'd try and make me do what he wanted me to do, but I was determined to challenge his authority. . . . Sometimes I'm amazed that I got through. I used to lie in bed and hold my breath, to try to die. Because I was so bad, it was the best thing to do.'

The family provides a perfect repository for more explicit domination in the form of violence. As a reasonably secure and private place, the home can become the stage where all the pent-up frustrations and emotions of other areas of life can be played out, generally on to other close members of the family. It is usually, although not necessarily, men rather than women who are violent within the family, either to wives/partners or children or both.[3] Men who have not achieved what they want to in the outside world of work or in social relationships, or have encountered frustrating experiences elsewhere, may use the family as a safe area in which to exert physical power. Consequently, there is the potential for a great degree of violence, whether it is expressed in verbal or physical ways.

What families see as 'acceptable' violence may vary enormously. In some, this means no physical punishment at all, and a look or psychological rejection can be enough; in others a clip round the ear, a belting or throwing things at one another may be a normal feature of daily life. Physical punishment may be seen as a last resort for some, but for others, extreme violence becomes a regular part of family life. In the last chapter, Sheila, aged twenty-nine, described how her father would praise her school achievements outside the family, but be cruel and unkind to her within it. She grew up in the northwest of England in the 1960s and 1970s. Her father was born in Ireland, a Catholic whose large family worked a smallholding. He had little education himself and came to England to work at the age of seventeen. Here he met his wife, and Sheila is the eldest of their five children. He was a violent father and she writes about their family life when she was young:

'I do have some happy memories of my father, of him playing with us and making jokes for us. He always worked hard to provide for us. Mostly though, I was frightened of him. He was extremely violent and unpredictable. He beat me when I was about six for using a tube of glue that he later needed. Being cheeky or naughty often led to a hiding. I can remember hiding in the wardrobe hoping he wouldn't find me. . . . I was a miserable child. At the age of eight my ambition was to go to boarding school; at the age of twelve my ambition was to be twenty-nine and have my own house and a good job. I always read a lot and read virtually any book I could get my hands on, it was an escape.'

Like many other children who experience violence or rejection from their parents, Sheila's reaction was to blame herself and believe that she was bad or wicked and the cause of everything that was happening:

'When I was first conscious of my father's violence, round about the age of six or seven, I felt it was my fault. That I was bad or ugly or perhaps adopted and that was why he didn't love me and was so cruel. I used to make bargains with God. If God stopped my father hitting us, I would make nine first Fridays – a peculiar Catholic ritual of going to mass and communion on the first Friday of every month nine times in a row – I would say the rosary everyday, I would be a nun when I grew up, I would go to Purgatory for extra time. After a couple of years of this I gave up and just hated him for what he was doing. I would not stay in the same room as him and for several years (from about twelve to sixteen) didn't speak to him. I couldn't bear to eat at the same table. I think this is quite significant really, food and meals being so close to love. I think my mother would've left but she couldn't support five kids by herself and the pressure from her Catholic family was in favour of staying. She did her best to protect us but it wasn't enough. . . . When I got to fourteen I told him to stop hitting me or I would go to the police and prosecute him. He never hit me again but still carried on hitting the others, although I tried to stop him. . . . My sisters once tackled him about it, asking him if he felt sorry for being so violent to us. His reply: "If you kids hadn't been so naughty I wouldn't have had to hit you."'

When Sheila was sixteen her mother took her and the other children into a women's refuge but her father persuaded her mother to bring them home. He blamed Sheila for trying to split them up. At eighteen she went to university where she felt in control of her life for the first time. She hardly went back home after that time and has seen little of her father since. He returned to Ireland, followed by her mother although they do not live together. Sheila changed her name to her mother's and felt she was making a new start. Now aged twenty-nine, she has achieved her ambition of having her own house and a good job; she has a partner and a daughter of eleven months, and a violence-free life. But she looks back with regret:

'There's a big gap in my experience of family life. I no longer hate my father, I feel sorry for him. I feel rather contemptuous of him but mostly I feel indifferent to him. I haven't seen him for three years and if I didn't see him again it wouldn't bother me. I find it hard to imagine why anyone feels love for their father, I can't imagine a normal relationship between a father and child or daughter yet I know it exists.'

Sheila does not feel she misses the relationship she has never had, in contrast to some women (such as Eve, quoted earlier) who have a strong sense of having been denied an important relationship. In this respect she shared the feelings of other women whose relationship with their fathers had more often been a physical absence from their lives, rather than a present but negative experience.

Another participant in a violent father–daughter relationship is Judy, who grew up with her parents and brother in the north of England. Her father was a bricklayer, her mother a housewife. Judy's parents had six children, and she was the firstborn. Sadly, four of her brothers and sisters had contracted a rare condition of muscular breakdown, and died when they were young. Only Judy and one brother survived. Obviously, this tragedy affected the whole family and Judy's memories of her father's violence coincide with, but are not necessarily caused by, these infant deaths. Their father was always a very dominating man and constantly tyrannised all members of the family:

'I think one of the first memories I have of him is him hitting me; and I can remember him dragging my mum literally bodily, trying to throw her out of the house. One of the babies was in the pram and she was trying to drag it out of the pram and he was snatching the baby back and throwing her clothes around. Those are my earliest memories. And him always going to the pub . . . he was so dominant. When I was fourteen or fifteen and wanted to start going out with my friends from school, he wouldn't allow it, so I had to lie. Once a week he'd let me go to the pictures with friends. But I never used to go to the pictures, I used to go to the rugby club instead! I was drinking under-age and being very silly, but it was wonderful to escape from the threat of violence – he only has to look at you now and he frightens. If he says "How much did that cost?" I won't tell him. I'm still frightened of him.'

Now in her thirties, Judy recalls her early memories of childhood and family life with her father:

'When he used to hit or beat me it was always a question of – close
all the doors, close all the curtains, check there was no-one out
the back because we lived in a terraced house, and then the
beatings would begin. We had a last meal as well. If he was going
to hit us he would always give us a last meal. It would always be
something really nice – though I'm vegetarian now – it would be
like chips and braising steak and gravy. I'd try and eat it as slowly
as I could. I remember belching as I was eating this meal with the
fear and anxiety. He'd just sit down one end of the room, reading
the paper and I'd be sat at the top with this tray on my knee,
eating little mouthfuls thinking, oh God, I want that meal to last
forever. Then when I'd finished that was that. Being a bricklayer
his hands were so huge and like leather, and so hard. He used
to hit me with his hand, it was awful. The bruising was just
tremendous. . . . When he hit me with his hands it was just this
barrage, he used to get so aggressive he used to be saying I'm not
going to stop till I put you in hospital. I'm not going to stop. He
would just completely lose control and mum would be trying to
drag him off and he'd be hitting her. When he hit me with a strap
sometimes it hurt but it was quicker and there was some control
whereas when he was just punching and hitting me, that was
frightening.

'He hit anywhere really, but never the face, my face was rarely
bruised. I used to get bruises on my body and there were times
when there was no way I could go to school, I used to have days
off school waiting for the bruising to go on my legs and back and
arms. I don't think you used to have to tell the school anything in
those days. It usually followed a parents' evening anyway. There
was one teacher that took an interest, I think she was the only one
who responded, the other teachers just hated me and I don't
blame them. She came to talk to me, she said she was going to
contact the NSPCC. I thought about this and I was absolutely
terrified because I knew I'd get beaten even more if he thought
I'd told anyone. So I went to her and said that about what I'd told
her before, that it was all lies. And she said "I thought so". Which
was awful. And then I just felt as if I didn't have any hope at all.
My dad had been so nice when she met him, she thought I had
just constructed the whole thing because I was such a naughty girl.

'He only stopped when I got married. Even then, I was still

frightened that he would hit me, he used to come down and threaten me. Even now the threat of physical abuse is always there. I know he can't do it I suppose, because I'd call the police, but I'm still frightened of him.'

Violence featured throughout Judy's life at home, and she became pregnant at sixteen, as she says, 'to escape my father'. She married her baby's father, a man much older than herself who also hit her. She had two children with him, but eventually could not tolerate him or his violence any more and divorced him. (She speaks more about this in Chapter 5.) Since then, largely through her own efforts, she has struggled to pursue education and get a degree, become a teacher and take control of her own life again. She has also remarried, but this time to a man who is gentle and considerate. Judy is an example of someone who has made great changes in her life and has broken what can, in other circumstances, turn into a cycle whose track grows deeper and harder to climb out from.

Violence between parents and children is a complicated issue. It is also tangled up with love, duty, discipline and power. A family does not have to be pathological to explode occasionally into some level of violence at a specific time, such as when children reach their adolescence and conflicts may erupt. Margaret and her sister grew up in a comfortable Jewish family home and she has a caring and close relationship with her father, Raymond. She was always his favourite. As a teenager, Margaret rebelled against her parents' expectations and this led to some dramatic and sometimes violent episodes between them. Raymond recalls these times:

'We had shouting matches, and I actually hit her. I don't think such violence would actually cause any harm at all. It's just that I felt it was the last straw and gave her a clip round the ear. I felt disappointed in her. I would like to have seen her better in her selection of friends and to make use of the home. I think every parent wants to see their children go along the same lines as they did themselves. When they start to go astray from the way you think they should, it gets under your skin and it tends to go wrong. I have to admit that through lack of patience I did tend to say "Right. I'm going to give her a wallop". And that was it. We had some traumatic times. My wife and I would literally sit down and cry.'

Although discipline ultimately came from both parents, it was communicated through Margaret's mother, and consequently

Margaret blamed her mother and defended the positive view she held of her father:

'I'd always blame my mum for everything, but my dad must have been in on it. I'm so protective of my father: he's the one who is really violent at times, and yet all the stuff that stopped me doing things, that was all through my mother. . . . Even the real violence and aggression was because he loved me. I never thought that he didn't love me. It was because he was so bound up in me and what I was doing that it created that, and I used to push deliberately. . . . I remember at the time, them wanting to wrap me in cotton wool, not wanting me to experience anything.'

Daughters with violent fathers may have to confront several contradictions: for instance, there may be a positive and loving side to their fathers, and their fathers may have both a public face and a private face. This makes it even more confusing to deal with all the mixed emotions of wanting to love someone who may occasionally show interest and affection but who is so cruel at other times. The extreme violence that Judy experienced from her father was described earlier, but he could also conceal this trait, and be surprisingly aimiable on occasions, as she describes:

'You never knew what mood he was going to be in, he could be just completely violent and horrible. But he would still sometimes do really nice things and you would think, oh he's not so bad, he can't help it, he loves me really. Or you'll have a nice conversation with him where he doesn't attack you in any way, and then it's just gone, lost, it's so confusing. There has always been this nice side to him and that's made it difficult as well. He had this public face and his home face.'

Love and violence are no strangers to one another, and some women who have experienced violence at the hands of their husband or partner claim that this is evidence of his love. It is very complicated if you are in a relationship with someone you love or you feel you want to love, but they are treating you in a cruel and violent way. Objectively, it seems logical to leave them but you cannot because you are still hooked into seeking their love and approval, however unforthcoming. Although Judy's father was extremely violent to her and her mother, she found herself maintaining a relationship with him even though she could not stand his violence and mental cruelty. After everything he had done, Judy still felt she loved him and wanted him to love and approve of her:[4]

'I have these very confused emotions. I think I've always loved him, and I think the problem has been I've always wanted him to love me and he's never really shown it in any way. He has this very sort of destructive love. I think love to him is totally controlling and hurting. He'll test loyalty by hurting you. Occasionally he would break down and cry which was the most moving thing. I remember once he was putting up the Christmas tree and he just broke down because of the children dying. I think when I've seen other men cry I've thought "You're pathetic", but even the thought of my dad crying makes me want to break down really, this hard man who's got so much emotion trapped inside him and it either breaks out like that which is fairly rare, or in violence. And he's never been really able to show that he loves anyone. . . . In the past it's always been hatred and anger, and me wanting to be loved. There's none of that now, I feel quite calm about it, but I feel upset. . . . I've got to stop striving for that relationship of wanting to be the little girl, wanting him to be affectionate, which won't come.'

Another example of paternal violence is the relationship that existed between Wendy, now in her late thirties, and her father, who is now sixty-two. Unlike Judy's situation, Wendy and her father have renewed a positive relationship, despite a period of violence in her teens. At this time she was unhappy at being a working-class girl attending a middle-class grammar school, and her parents' marriage was going through a bad patch. Wendy's father came to England from Ireland and went to work in the car industry when he was young. He married and had three daughters of which Wendy is the eldest. Wendy rebelled at school and there was a lot of conflict within the family. She writes:

'My father couldn't cope with my rebellion and at that time he was a rather violent man and we had some very nasty fights and arguments. If I knew of someone going through a similar situation now I would describe it as physical abuse. My father was also drinking heavily at this time and did so for about ten years which resulted in more screaming, shouting and fighting. So in all we had a violent unhappy few years at home. Yet I would have, and still do, defend my father in all situations, yet I despise my mother for what she's done to him. This is very difficult to explain, but I can sum it up by telling you that when my father was violent he always came back and said sorry, he always told me how much he loved me, etc. But my mother couldn't, she would be violent also but never repented, always maintaining that she was justified. I watched them fight and argue and my father always had to say sorry, whoever had started or created the situation.' Wendy would forgive her father for his actions, but not her mother.

Wendy left school and went to work in a bank. At nineteen she married to escape from home into a secure environment where she remained for nearly eighteen years:

'I pretended to be happy when I wasn't. I did what we had always done at home, pretended to the outside world that everything was fine, never talked about problems etc. I had two children, boys, my father's first grandsons, he was so proud. I remember "wanting a boy for my dad", which also reminds me of how I felt when taking the 11+ exam. I wanted "to pass for my dad".'

When the marriage broke down Wendy found her father more supportive and loving than she ever expected. Contributing to the change in their relationship has been her awareness of his underlying love and concern for her.

None of the violent experiences are ever mentioned within the family, but Wendy recognises how their relationship has improved, and how really dependent she now is on his love and approval:

'My father is a very important figure in my life. I went through years of confusion. But now he's calmed down completely. He doesn't drink, my parents are still together and happier now than they have ever been. Now I love him and I fear for my reaction to his death. He has had one heart attack ten years ago and is not a particularly healthy man.' Wendy's life has also changed in another way through her decision to go to college and take a degree, and she found her father equally supportive in this: 'I returned to study a few years ago and obtained a BA Hons in Social Studies last year. I chose when to be educated and I did it for myself, not for my dad. Again he was so proud of me and told me so. He makes me feel wonderful. I don't know if I'm still doing things for him. I don't think so, but I get great pleasure out of telling him about my achievements because I know he'll tell me he loves me and how proud he is of me and I love to hear that from him. Our relationship has changed. He doesn't dominate me any more. But I love him dearly and can forgive him everything he's ever done that hurt me. I don't understand it at all.'

Not surprisingly, violence at home has repercussions for children's behaviour inside and outside the family. Several women already quoted in this context describe how badly behaved they had been in school, or how they bullied the other children and had few friends. For example, Sheila recalls:

'At the age of six I started having behavioural problems at school – refusing to do work and sitting under the desk, disrupting classes by being loud and silly, fighting with other kids, eating books and paper, and I was referred to a psychologist.'

Judy's experiences at secondary school were similar:

'I was so naughty, I was horrible. I wasn't actually very popular at school, I was a bully. I'm only five foot now, and I remember going to the girls' grammar school because I was quite bright, and them being absolutely horrified with the way I behaved and my attitudes to everything. They knew my dad hit me because he would storm into school and say "Hit her, hit her!" giving his permission. So they knew, but I'm convinced that some of them took pleasure in it. They quite liked the fact I was going to get a good hiding for some of the things I'd done in school, but perhaps they didn't realise how serious it was.'

It is a very common reaction for children to feel responsible in some way for anything that has gone wrong in the family, whether it be parental separation, divorce, violence or rejection. This generates a lot of guilt, which is carried through into adult life. Judy had always held extremely guilty feelings, believing herself to have been a horrible child at home and at school, and therefore bringing things on herself. Thus she convinced herself that she deserved at least some of her father's punishment. Even with a second husband and new career, she finds it hard not to fear his dominant and destructive role in her life:

'I just feel so burdened with the past, all the guilt of it. I can't enjoy what I have now because I live in the past constantly. It's so difficult to shake it off. Like I've done such positive things with the kids I work with, but in the back of my mind is always this burden. I feel it's all going to disappear, it's all going to be taken away from me: something will happen, or dad will say something.

'I really expected him to phone up the headmistress and say "Do you realise that you've got a teacher who can't control her own children and who is an awful mother?" Because he does things like that and people believe him. So I feel it could all be snatched away from me. I've taken control [of my life] but whenever my mind dwells on it, it just all comes back, it's so powerful.'

It is largely through her own determination and strength that Judy has taken responsibility for her own life and found fulfilment through her job, husband and children, although there have been setbacks and problems along the way:

'I had to get on my own two feet. I think it was only when I came to that, that I could take control of my life, stop myself being abused, stop things happening to me, being a victim, and control my temper, try to rationalise. I am a more stable caring person, much more rational. I have little outbursts but they tend to be over quickly, not the devastating tantrums I used to have.'

It is said that violence breeds violence, and cycles of violence have been observed by which people reproduce the kind of violence that they experienced from their parents, within their own families. Such cycles of violence, like cycles of deprivation, may maintain such behaviour as much by the social and economic circumstances that people live in, as by a pathological personality. The interlocking factors operating can be very hard to unravel. A repeating cycle of violence was visible in Judy's family, and she describes the violence her father experienced at the hands of his own father:

'My father also has a history of very severe child abuse. He was almost branded by his father for stealing an apple and he was hit over the head with a poker and rendered unconscious. He was sent by his mother to take his father's suits down to the pawnshop "But don't tell your dad", and when he came back his dad would say "Where've you been?", and he couldn't tell him and his father used to beat him. So he has all that history. We've made excuses that he's been through a lot, but then so have we, and there comes a point where you can't excuse some of the things he does any more. He does know that he instils this terror in us, but by the same token he always says that compared to his dad, we've nothing to complain about at all, and that we should see some of the fellers at the pub whose wives get beaten every night without fail!'

Other fathers or daughters described similar repeating patterns. For example, Stanley, (father of Rosemary, quoted earlier) also experienced a violent upbringing but in this case his father was not around, it was at the hands of his mother. Rosemary recognises this aspect of her father's upbringing, and also how this had in turn affected her behaviour with her younger brother:

'My grandmother brought my dad up on her own, and that was a very close relationship, but she was violent towards him so he behaved towards me in the same way. I think she must have been making him feel wanted but also rejecting him, he must have learnt it somewhere, who knows where it started? He was very dominating and my way of surviving was to fight. My response was to be bad and be damned if I'd do what he wanted. He just wanted his own way in everything, and I learnt how to bully people from him. I was horrible to my brother, I used to beat him up. All I was doing was playing out what was done to me. I was constantly blamed for behaving badly, that I should be better and nice to my brother. It was impossible, and my brother hasn't forgiven me for that.'

Stanley acknowledges this:

'I was brought up to do as I was told, consequently I felt also that my children should do as they were told. We often used to have the fur flying. We often had shouting matches. I tend to raise my voice if I get excited. I suppose I have an idea that if I raise my voice enough then it will win the argument. I think losing my temper could be a safety valve although it doesn't do much for other people. I would at times chastise Rosemary in what I thought was the correct way. I didn't know any different, I did it the way I knew, the way I was brought up. I suppose all these things tend to build up your own character, and you let them out when you have children of your own.'

Although some families appear to pass down a cycle of repeated violence from generation to generation, this need not be so determined. Individuals can be as effectively repelled by parental behaviour as drawn to repeat it. For instance, Richard's relationship with his nineteen-year-old daughter Sophie has been quoted in various contexts as a very positive illustration in which there has been little need for discipline and punishment. Richard himself, however, came from a rather different kind of family, and he had been determined not to repeat his own father's violent behaviour. His father had been a devout Jehovah's Witness and tried, ultimately without success, to insist that his son become one as well, as Richard describes:

'I've spent a lot of my life trying not to be like my father. Whenever I'm aware that I'm behaving in a way that reminds me of him, I find it terrifying. I have tried to avoid repetition of him. If people didn't agree with him they were either stupid or just trying to annoy him. He saw a black and white world and what he believed was truth, if you didn't agree you were in error. I wouldn't suggest he was brutal or I was battered but if he thought that physical chastisement was necessary then he would give it out in very strong measure. He was a man on a very short fuse.'

This was confirmed by his daughter Sophie:

'His father was very heavy handed. I think that was one of the reasons my dad had this thing of never hitting me, because his father used to hit him, and he was determined he wasn't going to do that with me.'

There has been a lot of publicity and documentation about sexual abuse between fathers and daughters in the last decade or so since the initial findings of the Cleveland sexual abuse case. Although this is obviously an important area within the father–daughter relationship, it has already been well covered by other researchers[5] and therefore I did not make it a major issue within my interviews for this book. Consequently, I did not press the women I talked to as to whether they had experienced such abuse, and have collected little direct information on this. I felt that to do this could affect the nature of the interview and detract from the other underlying aspects of the father–daughter relationship that I wanted to tap. However, it was inevitable that some women spontaneously mentioned incidents of sexual abuse that had been experienced by themselves or by their sisters. One of these was Sheila, who earlier described her father's violence within the family, and their consequent estrangement. She had been devastated to discover much later that her younger sister had been sexually abused by her father when she was seven. She writes:

'He threatened to kill her if she ever told anyone, and he made her feel worthless, telling her she was fat, ugly and had yellow teeth. When she told me about it I was so sad, guilty, and angry all at once. So sad for her suffering that she'd been abused and frightened, and I'd been unable to help her; angry with him – I could have killed him – and I don't mean that lightly; and I felt guilty in case he had been getting back at me for standing up to him, because I'd threatened him with the police when I was fourteen and she was seven.'

This knowledge about her father's behaviour had made Sheila feel afraid for her own baby daughter:

'When I was pregnant I had nightmares about him harming the baby and not being able to stop it. Since she's been born I've been shocked by how fierce I feel about her, about protecting her and it is like feeling I have a second chance at childhood to experience it again. . . . The week [my sister] told me about the sexual abuse I wrote to him and said that because of the violence from him I didn't want him to have any contact with my daughter because I felt so strongly about protecting her. He wrote back pages of how he hadn't done anything wrong, nothing had ever been good enough for us and how we didn't behave properly.'

The feelings associated with such abuse, whether it is sexual or not, are quite similar, and Judy has noticed this parallel between other women's responses to sexual abuse and her own reactions to being physically abused by her father:

'He's never sexually abused me in any way but what I do find is, when I hear people talk about sexual abuse, their feelings are so similar to mine. All the feelings they felt about their fathers: the guilt, the anxiety, the secrecy, I could relate to all of that, and the fear of not being able to escape, and just the whole confused element of it.'

The media reporting on father–child abuse has not only affected the way women see men and the daughter–father relationship, but has also had repercussions on men's attitudes to their daughters. Several fathers I spoke to spontaneously commented on the way the publicity about the Cleveland case (and other cases) had made them cautious about their behaviour towards their daughters and young girls in general. One commented: 'People now feel that if you're an older adult male who enjoys the company of children, there is something perverted about you'; and another said: 'The fact that there is so much being talked about it puts a barrier up. You don't want to be seen to be over-demonstrative with a child and that's sad.' In one household, the twelve-year-old daughter was startled at her parents suddenly wearing dressing gowns due to their concern that she may mention their nudity to people at school and this might be misinterpreted. Men may feel irritated that at present they have to think twice before they cuddle their daughters in public, but at least this inconvenience will not radically affect their lives, unlike the guilt and anguish of children who have carried their childhood abuse secretly into adulthood.

If in this chapter I have tended to describe in detail some of the more extreme experiences of domination and violence that women have endured from their fathers, it is not to suggest that this is the most common experience. However, it does happen more frequently than we would like to believe, and was a prominent feature in the lives of a significant number of the women responding in my research. Violence physically embodies the potential power implied in male stereotypes and masculine personality characteristics. Although publicly condemned, aggression and violence still denote power in male terms, and this remains as a potential element in all relationships between men and women, inside and outside the family.

Chapter 4

Sexuality

'I never sat down with him and talked about boyfriends or sex or anything like that. I don't feel he would feel comfortable talking about it and I wouldn't feel comfortable.'

Jean

'I don't remember feeling guilty about having sex, because I think they wanted to know so much about my life and be in control of it that I used to enjoy doing the things that they didn't know about and keeping it secret, and feeling quite pleased. There was no mental privacy. I just felt so controlled.'

Margaret

'Parents have got a lot to answer for. It's a very complicated relationship. I think they have to be aware of allowing their daughters to be sexual beings. You can't separate it from what happens to women in society. We're supposed not to have real sexuality and power. Our sexuality is our power and it's frightening for them. They don't know how to handle it. It's very potent. My resistance to getting married, the ritual of my father handing over my sexuality to another person – I was acutely aware of that. There was no way he was in possession of my sexuality to be given away like that.'

Rosemary

Sex is definitely on today's public agenda. Most popular magazines and newspapers have a required quota of articles on every aspect of sex and sexuality, and the threat of AIDS has turned the spotlight even more brightly on sexual practices. Yet, within many families, discussion of this subject remains taboo or is diverted into jokes or oblique references. Some daughters may be sufficiently close to their mothers to talk in confidence but plenty do not, and find this even harder with their fathers. Whether the subject is periods, sexual intercourse, contraception or any other aspect relating to sex, parents often skate around the edge or do not discuss it at all. Many assume their children will be taught all they need to know at school and are content with this; some leave useful books strategically around the house; others breath a sigh of relief if, as they pluck up the courage to begin a prepared speech, they are told confidently that there is no need. There are some parents who manage to talk with ease and intimacy, but these are the minority. It is not just parents who have this reticence; children – and teenagers in particular – are often nervous and embarrassed about discussing such intimate subjects and are only too willing to collude in avoiding the issue, many believing they know it all already. Despite extensive media coverage of sexual issues, personal sexuality is a very private area and one where people prefer to expose their deeper feelings or vulnerabilities in a situation that feels secure and appropriate.

The liberal policies of the 1960s in relation to abortion and homosexuality, and the so-called permissiveness of this and the following decade, paved the way for at least some relaxation in sexual attitudes. Sex before marriage is now commonplace and illegitimacy no longer a taboo. Explicit sex scenes are now a regular feature in movies, and there is greater openness in discussing things like menstruation. These changes were reflected in only a minority of the father–daughter relationships that I encountered, such as in that of nineteen-year-old Sophie and her father Richard. They have always had a close relationship (see earlier chapters) and Sophie could be very open with both her parents:

'There isn't anything I don't talk about with them. I talked to both of them about going on the pill. Most of my friends I don't think could, certainly not to their dads. About things like starting periods, I think mum talked to me about it and I'd gone away and thought of lots of questions so I talked to dad. I don't remember it ever occurring to me to talk to my mum rather than my dad. It was just whoever happened to be around. And we've always wandered around partly dressed and we don't think about it. Before we had water in the house we used to have a tin bath like in those awful films, in front of the fire, so I've never been worried by that, it's very open. I think the general idea was you shouldn't be ashamed of your body so we just wandered around as we were.'

Her father Richard comments:

'It's a standing joke in the family, that I have suffered as much from pre-menstrual tension as anybody – at secondhand as it were! It's been a very real experience for me.'

Predictably, most of the older fathers that I talked to had very little role to play in whatever sex education was given to their daughters. If anything, their role was more confined to defining the family's moral position on sex before marriage, rather than explaining anything about what sexuality might involve. For instance, Raymond and his wife brought up their two daughters in a traditional Jewish family during the 1950s and 1960s. In common with many fathers then and now, Raymond was very relieved to relinquish this kind of responsibility, as he confirms:

'I left sex and sex education to my wife, she had a much better turn of phrase when doing anything of that sort. But I also did it because I suppose it was the easy way out. It might at that time have been a bit embarrassing for them. I thought it was something my wife would be much better to instill into them rather than myself. I often wonder whether it would have made any difference if I had.'

His daughter, Margaret, confirms this:

'Sex or morality, that was all from my mum. It was always silence from my father, apart from the rows, and "You don't have sex until you're married."'

Another example of a father from a similar generation is Stanley, whose close but violent relationship to his daughter Rosemary has already been well documented earlier. Now in his seventies, he grew up in a very strict family. He too had no wish to take part in his daughter's sex education, but he knew that his wife Gwen would not take on this responsibility either. He commented:

'I was brought up in a period when it was taboo to have anything said about sex at all, especially in front of young children. Parents tend to pass it on to their own children, but I don't think I ever discussed it in front of Rosemary. I often tried to get Gwen to discuss it with her but she wouldn't. . . . It wasn't the case that I couldn't talk to her, but being old-fashioned I didn't think it was a father's place.'

Nevertheless, Stanley did find himself having to answer some of Rosemary's childhood questions about sex and she recalls how the information she received was neither very clear nor reassuring:

'I think I'd seen my friend's "Visible Woman" which had a foetus, and a whole bunch of us had agreed that we'd find out from our parents how babies happened. There'd been an article in *Woman* about a woman who'd got pregnant and hadn't been married. Dad was busy, and I wheeled my dog out in the pram and said "How can women get pregnant if they're not married?" He said "Ah. Right". And he proceeded to tell me about the man inserting his member into the woman. And that I mustn't tell my mother that he'd told me. So I was part of a conspiracy then. What this "member" thing was – well, I had an idea but I wasn't sure, and it was the last thing I wanted anybody coming near to me with. My mother's sole contribution to my sex education was to tell me never to let anyone touch my privates. . . . When I was about seven I was assaulted by a man, he put his hand up my knickers. I didn't tell anybody about it for years and years. I didn't know it ever happened to anybody else. And it was their lack of giving me any information about it, and the fear that I would be blamed for what had happened that meant I never told them about it.'

It is easy to mystify and frighten children about sex by giving inadequate information. Years later, after Rosemary had been to university, she remembers her father telling her: '"I was worried that you'd end up getting pregnant and not be able to continue your studies." I said, "Did you think I didn't know anything about birth control?" and he said "Well, I didn't see any reason why you should or how you could have known anything." I said "Well, no, *you* hadn't told me anything, but I certainly made sure I knew." There was an awful lot of naïvety on his part, and lack of understanding or thought about what girls at that age were doing.'

Although both Raymond and Stanley are fathers from an older generation, many younger fathers today also avoid discussing sex with their children. It's not simply to do with generations: it's also linked to the level of intimate communication and the nature of relationships within the family. Tony and his fifteen-year-old daughter Laura have already illustrated the way fathers can withhold praise and approval from their daughters. Although they both feel they have a good relationship as father and daughter and they can chat together easily, this does not include discussions about sex, as she observes:

'My parents don't really talk about sex, my dad never, my mum sort of low key, it's quite amusing, under her breath really. My dad has never spoken to me about anything like that. If I wanted to go on the pill or something I'd probably talk to my mum. I couldn't talk to my dad. I think he'd be more embarrassed than me. My dad is for more everyday conversation. My mum is somewhat more intimate.'

For his part, Tony is well aware that sex education is an area into which he would rather not delve in conversation with his daughter:

'What a cop out – typical male chauvinist – I put women on a pedestal. I have not said anything [about sex]. I see it as female things. It's no big deal to me, everyone goes through it and they all come out the other side. Their chums are all in the same boat.'

Many fathers find it hard to talk about sex with their daughters, and to their sons may only make joking references or general statements about being careful. It may not be an easy topic for mothers but, in general, girls (and probably boys too) find it easier to confide in mothers and ask their advice rather than fathers. This partly relates to men's relative unease in talking about very personal issues, and the psychological distance that may exist between fathers and their children. Sex is about love, passion, emotion, anger and lots more. Women are, in general, far more used to expressing their feelings and find it easier to articulate the words to describe what they experience. Obviously there are sensitive and expressive men, and women who are unable to express feelings and emotions, but it is more often men who lack a language to do this and have little practice in this kind of communication. When boys or men talk amongst themselves about sex it is usually oriented much more to discussion of sexual process and performance, rather than feelings, anxieties and related problems.[1] To expose these is to expose vulnerability and thereby undermine their masculine image. Some men have a special friend or someone close in whom they can confide such anxieties, often an understanding female friend, but many do not.

Lacking the knowledge and practice of such intimate language means that fathers tend to 'cop out' (like Tony); give inadequate or intimidating information (like Stanley); or simply communicate a moral message such as 'No sex before marriage' (like Raymond).

Some parents may never talk about sex education, and others say things that are simply unhelpful. Finding the right words for sex education can be difficult between generations. Anne's father, for example, had no language to talk about sex with his daughter. She is in her early thirties, single and working as an advocate. When she was small, her four half-brothers and sisters from her father's previous marriage had all left home, so her childhood was spent mainly like an only child, and in the company of her father, a fireman. They were almost inseparable and excluded her mother from their activities. Anne tells of how her parents had actively avoided the issue of sex education until she was in her mid-teens, when her father suddenly felt an obligation to talk to her about sex and contraception. He wanted to voice his concern for her welfare, but the words he chose served only to upset her, as she describes:

'My mum never told me anything about sex. You know when you're at junior school you get these little cartoon books, well, I remember my mum nicked this off me – "You don't want to know about that." It was so excruciating, and then my dad gave me this lecture when I was about fifteen. He said "I want to talk to you." I said "What?" He said "If you get hot pants –" It's the most awful phrase! I didn't know what he was talking about at first. He said "I know your mother won't say anything to you so I want to make sure you go to a doctor". I thought he was calling me a prostitute. I was beside myself. I went upstairs really crying, I was so angry with him. And he was totally bemused. He was saying it, thinking he was doing the right thing, and then couldn't understand why I'm terribly upset.'

It is essential that there should be accessible alternative sources given in school, in literature and other media. Studies show that children know a lot about sex before they ever get sex education in school. However, many are under-informed or misinformed on certain essential subjects, but are too embarrassed or mistakenly confident to check out the accuracy of their knowledge.

Fathers in a two-parent family can pass this task over to mothers, but lone fathers caring for young daughters have little choice but to deal with issues of periods, boyfriends and sex in the best way possible. As with any family, the ease with which this can be accomplished will also depend on the openness within the parent-child relationship. Amongst the fathers and daughters I interviewed, Tom and his two daughters illustrate a single-parent family with a significant amount of openness. Tom, a teacher in his forties, is bringing up fourteen-year-old Paula and eleven-year-old Kim predominantly on his own. Although their mother does not live far away, they spend most time with their father. Consequently, for everyday needs around matters like periods they go to him, as Paula observes:

'We've had discussions about sex and most times we end up in fits of laughter. Sex is something we do talk about. I always go to my dad about things like periods. When I started, I was on holiday from school. I thought that's what it was, but I couldn't tell my mum so I told my dad. He said "Congratulations!" and he bought me a bracelet, so that was quite good. I go to my dad with most of that stuff. He's like a mum and a dad put together. He's the only one we can talk to about it.'

Kim adds:

'My friend's dad wouldn't tell her about sex or anything, he'd be too embarrassed, but my dad wouldn't. If I'm watching a programme on sex and I want to know more about how a baby happens or something, he'll get me a book. My mum gets embarrassed about that stuff, she wouldn't say anything to me.'

Tom's approach in talking about subjects like sex and contraception with his daughters was not to deliberately introduce the subject but to let it come up in conversation:

'When children ask about these things, or mention them, it's a clue, a code for saying "Tell me more, I don't know". Some children keep things secret from their fathers and I'm sure that's to do with the way a lot of children pick up coded messages from their parents about taboo topics of conversation.'

Peter is another illustration of single parenthood, in this case with a part-time responsibility for his fourteen-year-old daughter Melanie, who lives with him in his flat every other week. Aged thirty-eight, he works in building maintenance but is studying to be a surveyor. His experiences living in a communal house in the

1970s with Melanie's mother have made him aware of feminism and shared childcare, and conscious of sex roles. Nevertheless, he and Melanie have tacitly relinquished the subject of sex to her mother:

'I don't think I'd have many problems talking to her about sex, if that's what she wanted to know, but I think she talks about it more to her mother than to me, because she's a female. We talk about love more than sex. I think sex is still very dark and not very pleasant for her. Having said that of course, if she asked me a lot of stuff about my sex life maybe I would clam up. It's a matter of finding the right words and the right context for it all.'

The right words and the right context are often very difficult to come by, and Peter touches on an important point when he says he might be reluctant to discuss his own sex life. Talking about sexuality to your children can also imply some potential exposure of your own personal experiences. Many parents would find this hard to do and therefore consciously or unconsciously avoid creating such an opportunity. They do not want to appear as sexual beings to their children, any more than their children really want to be made aware of their parents' sexuality. It is an area of potential vulnerability on both sides and testimony to the need for sensitive and accessible sex education outside the family. It is also important to look at the way sex is communicated to daughters within the family in terms of risk and danger, rather than the possibility of choice and pleasure. Parents feel the need to warn their children against sexual activity, and neglect to suggest they might enjoy it.[2]

As lone parents, Tom and Peter have each taken an equal or major role in their daughters' lives since they separated from their partners. In contrast, David, now in his sixties, has been more like an absent father in most of the life of Fiona and her two sisters after he divorced her mother and remarried. It was her mother who took responsibility for any sex education and rules about going out with and sleeping with boys. David was not even aware that Fiona had boyfriends. Even if David had been present more in Fiona's earlier life, it seems unlikely that he could have taken on the subject of sex education. He takes the view that it would be much better not to have to talk about these things in families at all, but to have a surrogate parent you can discuss them with. He believes real fathers are far too bound up with the complicated feelings they have for their daughters, as he explains:

'If you have a sort of substitute father, in many ways he may be able to do the things that the father wanted to do but couldn't, because of clots of emotion and feelings stirring about in the atmosphere. You don't know what's going on inside these creatures and you have to move carefully. Then you could talk, you could ask advice on things like sex somehow by the fact that you haven't had all this tremendous intimacy. Funnily enough, you would think if you'd wiped somebody's bottom a thousand times it might make it easier but it doesn't. I can talk about sex in general, about other people's sex, but I never really got to talking about that with Fiona. I never did with my other daughters . . . and in some ways you've got no more right than to go and ask the girl next door what she's doing.'

In many ways he is right, and it is very often easier for a young person to talk about intimate issues with someone who is not as closely related as a parent.

In most families discussion of personal and sexual topics generally falls to women, clearly seen as 'women's issues' and endorsed by their abundance in women's magazines. It has traditionally fallen to fathers to define the family morality, in keeping with the patriarchal role of power and authority. Implicit or explicit, this moral message will be clearly understood within the family. Since attitudes to sexual morality have relaxed over the last few decades, it was no surprise to find that the older fathers I spoke to generally held stricter views about sexual behaviour than younger ones. Sometimes this stems from religious beliefs, but for many it harks back to an era when sexual taboos were strong. Stanley grew up in this era, and has described his views on sex roles and sex education earlier. A retired insurance salesman, he had high aspirations for his daughter, but he also had over-riding concerns about sex before marriage:

'My mother had a saying "It's the boy's place to try but the girl's to deny." And it's something that I've always had with me. I have the idea that no-one should have sex until they get married. That is my idea of life and something I would have preferred as far as Rosemary is concerned. I had a fairly strict upbringing, and I was quite strict with her about what time she should be in and the rest of it. I suppose it's the inborn fear of scandal as much as anything else as far as a girl is concerned. It was *infra dig* for a girl to have a child out of wedlock and this was a fear I had in the back of my mind with Rosemary and her boyfriends.'

Rosemary was part of the generation that was passing through its teens and twenties in the late 1960s and 1970s – the 'pill generation', who took advantage of this freedom to explore sexuality without the commitment of marriage, within the safety of reliable contraception, and rejecting the morality that had previously predominated.

Morality is a form of social control, and in this case it dovetails with the control that many parents (fathers in particular) would like to retain over their young daughters. For a father this is not only to do with protection, but also with preserving his daughter's virginity. Maintaining her childhood innocence keeps her from the (sexual) influence of another man. Stanley's fears for his daughter's virginity were realised when she left home for university:

'I suppose you cannot rule any child's life, and they're going to leave the nest some time and once they go to university that's the end of it. While she was at university, obviously there was nothing I could do about it. It's obvious she was no longer, shall we say, a virgin. She decided to go off with one of the blokes and they used to live together. I felt hurt, it was like an act of defiance, especially when she knew I wouldn't approve. I felt very sick about it, very unhappy. I suppose I felt somewhere along the line I had failed her. Being me, I didn't like to blame me for it, although if there was anyone to blame it was obviously me, although I don't suppose it would have made any difference if I had discussed the matter with her during adolescence or not. I still think that Rosemary would have gone her own way.' For Stanley, his daughter Rosemary's sexual initiation was not just her loss but a personal loss to himself: 'I realised then that although she was still my daughter she was on a different level, it felt more separate. Although it possibly didn't make any difference to her, it wasn't the same to me, I'd kind of lost her.'

Although Stanley did not succeed in preventing Rosemary from having a sexual relationship, the dominating nature of his moral views had a lasting impact on her feelings about sex. She could not just dismiss his reactions and attitudes, not only because he was her father but because her closeness and identification with him when she was small meant that she took on his view of her and he was the only one who could forgive her for being 'bad'. Now thirty-eight and expecting her first child, Rosemary describes her early memories:

'I was thirteen and going out with spotty Brian, my first-ever date. I was waiting for him to turn up and my dad came in. He looked ever so serious and said "I must have a word with you." Then he gave me this whole lecture about how I had to stay a virgin until I got married. I thought this is crazy, and I kind of said "Mmm". But that sat in my head. So any kind of amorous encounters as an adolescent, always my father was sitting in my head. It was just unbearable, it took ages to get it out of my head. It didn't stop me having sex, but it did mean I didn't really think very clearly about what I needed for me, and ended up sleeping with some-body when I was eighteen. I didn't really like him and I was actually quite frightened of him. I didn't tell him I was a virgin and I was terrified I'd get pregnant because I didn't have any contraception. I was just frozen, but I felt that I was damned if my dad was going to stop me. It had exactly the opposite effect instead: defiance. Being pregnant now, I realise that I have still actually taken on board his morality, even though I ignored it and denied it and went completely in the other direction. It is still sitting in me, I was still a bad wicked woman. I'd done something wrong.'

A father's perception of his daughter is complicated by several related factors, such as possessiveness; a desire to preserve her innocence; and the implicit threat presented by male com-petition for their daughter's affection and attention. Stanley's attitudes are rooted in patriarchal control of women's sexuality by which women represent the property of first their father, and then their husband on marriage. Daughters belong to fathers twice over, as children and as females. In a traditional patri-archal society where property is passed down through the family, it is important to control who women have children with, and therefore crucial that unmarried daughters are virgins and wives are faithful. Although this is no longer a prevalent concern in British society, it is still tangled up in male attitudes to women. It contributes to Stanley feeling that he has 'lost' Rosemary through her loss of virginity, and that he has somehow failed in his ability to control her. He also felt he had failed in his role as protecter.

Whether fathers are defining morality for their daughters from a religious or personal perspective, they are employing an age-old view of the virgin versus the whore. This concept is well docu-mented in religion, art and literature. It polarises femininity: the whore represents the woman with whom men may enjoy sexual experiences, while the virgin is the woman they marry or with whom they select to spend their life. This double standard splits women into two opposing stereotypes and objectifies both of them. There is no parallel for men.

Similarly, the denigration of girls, implied in being called a 'slag' for their reputed sexual activities, has no recognised equivalent for men.[3] There are other related differences: for instance, a girl's loss of virginity is usually seen as a significant event, but referring to it as a 'loss' denies any pleasure or gain in status, unlike the equivalent for boys. Men's sexual initiation is a rite of passage and proof of manhood, but the equivalent does not hold for girls. Motherhood is seen to confirm womanhood for girls. A father's anxiety about his daughter's sexuality and her innocence is not simply concerned with her own safety and welfare. It has many other complex threads that lead back inside men to aspects of power and control and to male attitudes to the 'violation' of women. One woman now in her forties recalled an incident that happened about twenty years ago, when her father discovered she was having a sexual relationship. He became really angry, called her a whore, said she was 'shop-soiled', and threatened to hit her boyfriend. We may like to dismiss fathers like this as out-dated and over-reacting, but they still exist. Such words and reactions reflect assumptions that still underpin men's attitudes to women and sexuality today and influence fathers' relationships with their daughters.

Fathers' concern to preserve their daughters' innocence and the fear of losing them to other men reflects sexual jealousy and possessiveness. It may also contain some fear of female sexuality and its potential power over men. One woman wrote describing how protective her father was of her when she was a teenager: he never allowed her to stay out with her friends and he also tried to stop her wearing adult clothes: 'I remember when I wanted to start wearing tights. I was the only one left in socks and he was arguing with my mother and said "Next thing you know she'll be pregnant!" I never understood his attitude.' This attitude has a familiar ring. It expresses the simple logic that says if young girls dress in a sexually mature way they will attract men and be taken advantage of by them. This attitude expresses fathers' fears for their daughters and their own sexual fantasies; or perhaps recalls sexual experiences or aspirations they had in their youth. What they considered permissible behaviour for the girls they encountered at that time is unthinkable in their daughters. It is a double standard, like that of the whore and the virgin. Part of the image we give to sex has a raw, dark, uncontrollable side to it, separate from love, and perhaps contains men's fears of being controlled by women's sexual power. The extent to which men may be afraid of their daughters' sexuality is another aspect of their concern to control it.

If trying to prescribe and enforce sexual morality has proved a problem, then coming to terms with the onset of their daughter's sexual activity creates even more. One father commented: 'I always hoped sex would not rear its ugly head until they got married.' The possibility of sex exists as soon as girls start to go out with boys. Sex equals danger in the minds of many fathers when it comes to teenage daughters. Tony (quoted earlier) is one such father, who has not yet had this to confront with his teenage daughter Laura. She has a steady boyfriend but as yet it is not a sexual relationship, and Tony does not care to dwell too deeply on this aspect. He prefers to see it as a 'harmless' friendship, and comments:

'She's been going out with him for a long time. It's not a serious relationship, it's a comfortable relationship and they get on well. They chat more like a couple of girls. I don't think there's anything heavy in it, by that I mean serious or sexual. I don't know about the sexual part. I don't really like to think about that, fathers don't, because I know what I was like at that age, I was interested in girls early . . . but the relationship that Laura has doesn't worry me.'

Tony knows that he would find it difficult to accept if he thought sex was involved and Laura is well aware of this. In common with many other daughters, she will probably end up protecting him and herself by not telling him, with the collusion of her mother:

'I think my dad would find it hard if he thought I was having a sexual relationship. I think he sees me as his little girl still. Every time I'm introduced to somebody he sort of hugs me and says "This is my little daughter". I can come out with all kinds of crude jokes but I still think he sees me as innocent. If I did [have a sexual relationship], I think it would be a "Don't tell dad" really. I think it would embarrass him, he wouldn't know what to say, whereas mum would level it out, give me all the lectures and things. But I couldn't tell my dad, I don't know why.'

Clearly part of the reason she could not tell her father is related to her father's message that he wants to continue seeing her as his innocent little girl. In their collusion, mother and daughter here combine to produce the reverse situation – they are keeping father innocent of the fact that his 'little girl' is no more. In the end, whose innocence are they really protecting?

The strength of men's feelings about their daughter's sexual behaviour may erupt in sudden and aggressive behaviour. Fathers who have maintained an image of their daughter's innocence and who are possessive about her affections and her sexuality, and those who have strong moral or religious views on sex, find it very traumatic to discover that their young daughter has a sexual life of her own. Reactions can be angry and violent. An incident between Lesley and her father Bob illustrates this. As an only child, Lesley was closer to her father than her mother when she was small, but this changed in her teens, when her relationship with her mother took a more prominent role. Bob did not hold particularly strong religious or moral views, but he was taken off guard when the innocent image of his teenage daughter was suddenly shattered. She recalls the occasion:

'My dad did catch me out one day. He went to do something and dropped me and the dog off. And there were these two guys and we were on the grass, rolling about and the other guy was playing with the dog and Dad came up. He was really disgusted. I felt terrible, guilty and ashamed. I'm not sure whether it was because he'd seen me with a man – his daughter – and he wanted to protect me. He was so angry that he hit me. Something he had never done, something I never associated with dad.'

In another normally peaceful family, seventeen-year-old Helen discovered that having a sexual relationship eventually provoked an unprecedented level of anger and aggression in her father. Helen, a music student, and her father Graham, who teaches music, normally had a warm and close relationship. Both her parents have strong religious beliefs about pre-marital sex and were upset when they found Helen was sexually involved with someone of whom they did not approve. They tried to stop her seeing him but Helen refused. This and her continuing sexual relationship with this young man could not be easily accommodated by her father. The relationship created tension between Helen and her parents and she vividly remembers one violent episode:

'I decided I was moving out to be with Paul and I was packing my bags to go for a couple of days. I'd locked my room because I wanted to be private, mum and dad were outside, then dad burst the lock and came storming in and hit me round the face and I hit him back. My poor mother was trying to separate us. He was crying and so was I.'

Although Helen and her boyfriend did eventually split up, the whole family was traumatised for many months by the impact of this relationship. Ultimately both sides, caring deeply for each other, came to recognise the other's position. This was made easier by Helen's move to college at eighteen, which confirmed her autonomy and independence for herself and in the eyes of her father. Although Graham still holds strong religious and moral beliefs about sex, he has recognised that Helen has matured as a result of her experiences: 'Now I respect her as an adult. She is prematurely an adult if you like, partly because she's lost her virginity.' Many fathers, including Graham, find it hard to say this about their teenage daughters at the time it is happening.

Such extreme and negative attitudes and reactions to daughters' sexuality are also intricately linked with fears about pregnancy. Pregnancy is the product of a sexual relationship, visual proof of sexual activity from a daughter who is no longer innocent. Some fathers react strongly to the discovery that their young daughter is pregnant, as though she (and in some way they too) has been violated. Consequently, teenage pregnancy may come as an equal shock to both parents, but it is generally mothers who recover fastest and are usually more immediately supportive and helpful to their daughters. Fathers often have a more extreme reaction and tend to maintain this anger for longer. Some feel hurt and betrayed by their daughter's revelation; they may refuse to speak to her for several weeks or more. Teenage girls themselves are usually far more frightened of telling their fathers than their mothers. They know that fathers often have more extreme attitudes to boyfriends and sexual activities than mothers do. It is therefore mothers who usually have to break this particular piece of news to husbands or partners.[4] Fathers who feel jealous about their daughter's sexuality are now forced to recognise that she has been sexually active with another man, and watching her grow larger as the pregnancy progresses may increase their negative reactions. It is interesting that some teenage mothers describe how angry and rejecting their fathers were during their pregnancy, but how they are transformed into caring fathers after the baby is born. Perhaps when their daughter is back to her normal size they can ignore her sexuality again, and the new baby provides a non-sexual distraction and the novel experience of grandfatherhood.

In contrast to some of the possessive reactions described, nineteen-year-old Sophie has found her father Richard to be very reasonable about her boyfriends, and her current boyfriend now lives with her and her parents:

'He moved in when my dad was away studying, and it was very awkward at first. He'd got on with my mum and everything was fine, then my dad came back and there was a bit of friction. Not that they ever fell out but they didn't talk to each other a lot. Dad said "I hope I'm not being a possessive father and being jealous". I don't know what it was, but it's a lot better now. Maybe it was everything being done without them getting to know each other gradually. And I obviously spent less time with dad, I felt torn, and I do even now sometimes.'

Richard is not aware of any jealousy about Sophie's boyfriends:

'I didn't feel jealous when she started having boyfriends, quite the reverse really. In a way that was part of her growing up. In any case, I've had different relationships with women and she needs to have different relationships with men. The one she has with me is, for better or worse, unique, whether it's good or bad, that's her father–relationship, she can't have another one. So I don't feel in any way intimidated by it. Obviously, some of her boyfriends I haven't entirely approved of, but that's more in the sense that I don't particularly relate to them. There's some I felt comfortable with and others I didn't.'

Compared with many other fathers, Richard is very open in his attitude towards his daughter's sexuality, to the extent that he was concerned that they were not yet having a sexual relationship. Sophie recalls:

'Simon and I had talked and we thought, yes, I'll go on the pill. But I didn't want to do it until I talked to my parents. Not to get their opinion, because we'd already decided, but just to let them know. I think I'd have felt a bit guilty about doing it behind their backs. I was about eighteen. I know my dad was surprised that I hadn't said anything about it before, but I think it would have been embarrassing for Simon sooner. We were sleeping in the same room but we had separate beds whereas now we've got a double bed. I'm sure it must be strange for my parents having me and Simon having a sexual relationship here, but they never say so, which is nice, I feel I can do what I want to do.'

A father's recognition that his daughter is a sexual person in her own right can help her to develop confidence in her own sexuality and confirm her sexual identity. Many women are convinced that their father's attitude to sex, and their daughter's sexuality in particular, had affected their later relationships with men. Lisa was one of these. Now thirty-one, she received little reassurance about her feminine identity within the family. She is an only child and grew up in the northwest of England. Her father was a skilled manual worker and her mother trained as a teacher. She felt her father always saw her as a problem and never really felt comfortable with her. She writes, recalling the change in their relationship with the onset of puberty:

'My parents gave me no positive reinforcement about my image or appearance. I was just a "funny girl". If things had been less than ideal at home for my first twelve years, they now became really tempestuous. A new form of teasing arose and the subject was boys. Dad lost few opportunities to tease me about my burgeoning sexuality and what he imagined I would soon be doing with boys. This early association of sex with embarrassment undoubtedly affected my later sexual relationships.'

It is one thing for fathers to acknowledge and confirm their daughter as a sexual person, but another to desire them. Fathers are not meant to desire their daughters. Yet if men's view of women is essentially a sexual one, this is always a possibility. It is an uncomfortable question that cannot be ignored. Men cannot help but notice if their daughters are sexually attractive, and usually appreciate this observation. Peter for instance, a part-time parent whose reticent role in sex education was quoted early in this chapter, had recently become aware of his fourteen-year-old daughter as a good-looking young woman:

'The way she looked the other day, I sort of saw her as halfway desirable for the first time. It wasn't about lust or desire or sex or anything like that. It was more like you'd look at an old friend and think that, and then dismiss it, and yet it was definitely there. I guess that might lead into something more like jealousy if she started seeing boyfriends later on. Talk to me in two years time and I'll tell you more about it!'

The incest taboo generally distances sexual desire, and replaces it with a distaste for such unacceptable feelings. The point when fathers become aware of their daughters growing more physically mature, and essentially more sexual, often coincides with a process of withdrawal. Where fathers may have played and tumbled in a physical way with their daughters, they now feel the need to preserve a sense of distance. This can feel like a form of rejection to a daughter whose sense of herself as physically or sexually mature does not necessarily coincide with her father's.

Where paternal desire exists, it is usually controlled by the taboos around family incest. But clearly a significant number of daughters are sexually abused by their fathers. The inbalance of power between parent and child and the tangled emotions of love, hate and guilt involved make it hard for girls who have been abused to tell anyone what has happened, or even admit it to themselves. Fathers who do express even mild physical desire to their daughters are on dangerous ground and can swiftly confuse, threaten and alienate any positive aspects of the relationship they already have with their daughters.

This may not only happen in childhood. One woman wrote to me describing how her father had expressed sexual feelings for her after she was grown up and had left home. Yvonne was an only child who grew up in the north of England. She had a contradictory relationship with her father when she was a child. He was fun to be with, she was devoted to him, but he could also be very unkind and there was a more suspect side to him as Yvonne describes:

'When I grew up he still put me down a lot but I became immune. However, he found it easier to be demonstrative, to the extent that he wanted to make love to me! He thought it was natural for father and daughter to make love and could not understand why I disagreed. Maybe it is natural for a father to have these feelings but he shouldn't have told me! If we were alone in the car he would touch my leg, say "I turned him on" and other things which made me feel uncomfortable. My mother said he was only joking and I was exaggerating. Luckily by this time I was not living at home any more so I could avoid being alone with him most of the time.'

If it is such a problem for some fathers to accept another man coming into their daughter's life, perhaps it is less of a threat if she has relationships with women instead. Having a daughter who is lesbian is likely to be a more acceptable than having a son who is gay. It is more like welcoming the partner as another daughter into the family. This is how it appears for David (quoted earlier). The youngest of David's four daughters is a lesbian, and he finds it easier to relate to her female partner than he would to another man:

'When her mother first said to me "You do realise she's a lesbian?" I said "Are you sure?" I immediately went and talked to her about it and I was prepared for some sort of feeling in myself, because I am a creature of how I have grown up, so that I might find it extreme and so on. But after two minutes it seemed to be perfectly normal. Her girlfriend comes and stays here. If anything, I'm warmer to them because they are two girls and I am able to put my arms round them, than I would be to a daughter with a husband, who is immediately slightly distanced from me.'

Sexuality is not an easy subject of conversation between parents and children and, in Lesley's case, this involved deciding to tell her parents she was a lesbian. An only child, she spent much of her childhood in the company of her father, and earlier in the chapter she describes his violent reaction to finding her with a boy. As a teenager, Lesley had boyfriends and sexual relationships with men, but when she had her first sexual experience with a woman she found it so much more fulfilling that it totally changed her life. At first she said nothing to her parents, but one weekend her mother approached her about it:

'My mother guessed that I was involved with another woman when I was twenty-two and asked me outright. I didn't admit to it initially. I told her later the same day and she was great. She wanted to know all about it and yet she didn't want to know, she was really torn. She didn't know quite what to think. She's pretty good, she actually tells friends that I'm lesbian now. She advised me not to tell dad then – not for a while. A year later, the day after I moved in with my then current lover, mum told dad about my sexuality. She thought if we told him before he might not help me move! She hadn't got a clue how he would react. She had a feeling he might be really anti because of his experience in the navy. I wasn't actually there when she told him. Apparently his

initial verbal response was "So what? She's still my daughter."
He's never treated me any differently. He has shown concern
inasmuch as he says "You don't hold hands or anything in public,
do you?" because he thinks we'll get beaten up I suppose. I can
talk to him about it. I mean, he's not for it, but he thinks live and
let live basically. All I know is as far as he's concerned, as long as
I'm happy with whatever it is I'm doing, then that's fine. I think
he's only been concerned in the past because it's not socially
accepted. . . . Dad's never said anything. I think it might bother
him more if it was a bloke that he didn't like. He's never had to
give me up to some other man, so it's different.'

Lesley's father Bob himself describes his contact with homosexuality during his time in the navy, when he was required to give
evidence after discovering other men participating in this. Although
he has reservations about lesbianism, he has enough love for his
daughter to respect the sexual decisions she has made about her
life:

'When she told us she was a lesbian – she told my wife Joan first
– we talked it over, all three of us. Joan accepted it, well she had
to. We have talked about lesbianism a lot. I think the only natural
union is between a man and a woman. You get other things on
the fringe and lesbianism is one of these. Lesley says it's not
something you voluntarily do, you just find you are. She started
out with boys, and she finds the relationship with women sexually
and normally is a much closer relationship, which is fair enough.
I think lesbianism is more acceptable than homosexuality, although
sometimes when she starts talking about dykes and that, I don't
think they could pick worse words because then you're thinking
of your daughter as an "old dyke". This brings the associations
right home to your doorstep. I've been to some of the gay pubs
and places with Lesley, where they're hanging around to pick
someone up. To me that's a different kind of lesbianism than I
like to associate with my daughter, although I'm quite prepared
to take on board a one-to-one relationship in that respect.'

Since many fathers find it difficult to acknowledge the sexual
activities of their daughters, particularly when they involve sexual
intercourse, perhaps a lesbian relationship is easier to come to
terms with because it does not imply penile penetration. For men,
sex without penetration can rarely be classified as 'proper' sex.
This may make the physical aspects of the sexual relationship more

acceptable. Lesley often takes her girlfriends to visit her parents at their home. She comments:

'They have both been very supportive and accepted my lovers over the years. We've been able to stay at my parents in a double bed, bathe together and show affection – even though my parents are embarrassed when confronted by my lover and I having a cuddle! Mum said the way she's accepted it, she sees us as two close friends, although she finds it hard to cope with trying to think about the physical aspect of it.'

It is tempting to look at childhood experiences or relationships to find clues that might explain why one person is gay and another is not. Perhaps these indicators do exist, but research is not consistent on this question, and the many influences on our sexual development are not so simply defined.[5] Lesley herself reflects on this question:

'I think it might have been my unconsciously thinking I don't want to live like they do. I suppose all the time in my teens, even my twenties, I just thought I don't know anybody that's happily married, and nothing interested me about marriage. At one point I did want to get married, when I was sixteen, to this guy in his forties, but I was soon talked out of that one. I was in relationships most of the time but I just couldn't get close to men at all.' The latter is an experience not uncommon to women in general.

The restrictions imposed within families from cultures with strict religious beliefs often give girls little freedom. In Asian or Cypriot communities for instance, the family is concerned to protect daughters from contact with boys and and eventually ensure that she has a good marriage. The family's reputation may be at stake if she resists. This usually means keeping a daughter's virginity intact until she is married, or at least making it appear that way.[6] Maria is nineteen and comes from a Greek-Cypriot family. Her father was born in Cyprus and has lived here since he was twelve. Like many girls in such strict communities, Maria was not meant to go out with boys but she did, negotiating this with her mother. She had her first boyfriend at fourteen but kept this from her father by going around in a group, and arranging that her father would always collect her. He gave Maria's mother the responsibility of warning her against boys, saying 'If anything happens to her it's your fault', so her mother was reluctant to let Maria go out. This provoked rows between them, but never as great as those Maria has had with her father about boys. She recalls one occasion:

'I went out with Terry, who was about four years older than me and had a car, and we got lost. I got back about one or two o'clock. I didn't think Dad would be waiting for me but he was, and he shouted at me, he even hit me. It really hurt. I felt awful and I cried a lot. I made him feel sorry for me. We didn't speak to each other for a few days. That's the one time he's really got involved, usually it's just through my mum. I think he was trying to protect me, he probably thought I was doing something really bad. He was angry and let it all out. I think it's more his Greek side, the fiery side of him. He's really thinking of what his mum would think, probably his family reputation at stake.'

Maria's family reputation is still in the foreground now that she is engaged. Her fiancé, also Greek-Cypriot, has moved into her family home. Although she has no qualms about having sex before marriage herself, she outwardly conforms to the expectations of her father in this respect, and she and her fiancé have separate rooms:

'It's because of my dad that we're doing it. We haven't argued about it because we like to respect his views. It's my mum as well, but my mum's doing it for my dad. He's really against all that. He's made it clear to everyone in Cyprus that we're not in the same room, even though we're in the same house now . . . It makes no real difference whether we have sex before marriage and I think he knows that as well, but I think he just doesn't want to show everyone, and I understand that.'

When Maria had told her father she was planning to marry at nineteen her father objected because she had only known her boyfriend for three months and he had no steady work, but Maria was determined and in the end he came to terms with it:

'I knew he was annoyed but we didn't discuss it. He wanted to sort it out himself. He wanted to go and see my fiancé's father and mother and sort it out with them, see what they thought about it. He was dead against it, mainly because Andy hadn't got a job at that moment, and because I was his daughter I think, so young and it happened too fast for him. He gets on really well with Andy now, but the first six months were really bad. Then Andy got a job, and in the end, we had a rushed engagement in November and everyone was fine about that. It was my eighteenth birthday.'

Maria believes that the hardest thing for her father to accept was that he felt he was losing her:

'At the beginning, my dad couldn't take it. He couldn't stand losing his daughter I suppose. All my relatives used to come round and there used to be endless arguments amongst them. We used to stay in the other room. Dad used to say "She's so young!" and everything. They used to come in and say "Don't worry. He's just scared of losing you." And that's what it came down to. It's funny that he feels he'll be losing me because I'll only be living round the corner. But I won't be living here, and he won't be in charge. I'll have a husband, so he won't have a say in what I do any more. All his control was over me, and now he won't be able to do that.' Her father's control of her has been somewhat of an illusion and certainly a struggle, but it is an illusion in which the family colludes.

Similar pressures exist to protect girls and organise their marriage in families from other cultural backgrounds, such as in Asian families. For those families who have lived in England for many years, the rules around arranged marriage may have been loosened, or even abandoned altogether. Where marriages are still arranged, there is usually more opportunity for a girl to meet with and decide if she likes the man her parents have chosen. If not, she will say so and they will find someone else. Sonika, for example, had an arranged marriage nearly two years ago. Her father works as a carpenter and Sonika, aged twenty-three, has a job as a secretary. At seventeen, her parents wanted to find her a husband, but Sonika managed to put them off until she was twenty-one. Her husband is thirty-two. She recalls:

'When I was seventeen, at college, my dad said to me "We're going to start looking for somebody." I said "Not yet, not until I'm twenty-one." I thought I could have fun, it seemed ages then. But when I became twenty-one my dad says "Right, we're definitely looking for somebody now." I wanted to wait a couple more years, but he said "No", because the older you get the harder it is for the parents to find you a boy. So I thought, I'll have to be ready now, so that was it.' Now that she is married and this family pressure is gone, it has been replaced by that to produce children. She observes:

'I think my parents will be happy when I have children. My cousin will be having a kid this month, so I think my mum and dad are thinking "When is she going to have one?" First you get the pressure that you have to get married, and then the next pressure is having kids. When my dad goes to the temple, people say "How is your daughter? Any good news?" But I think I want to work first. When the family are round they say "Any good news?" so I say "No. No good news, but I've seen a really nice cot."'

Sonika described her relationship with her father (and mother), as not being very close, and communication awkward at times, but she admits to a particularly strong affection for her father, and misses him now that she is no longer living at home.

Marriage and motherhood is the traditional route by which women leave the family and gain adult female status. They also leave their fathers, as Maria and Sonika have done. It can be very difficult for fathers to accept their daughters as independent adult women rather than little girls, and some never do. Separation can be promoted, however, by physical separation, for instance, if daughters go away to college, or work abroad, or if they marry. Marriage is a symbolic ritual representing the handing over of a daughter, by her father, to the keeping of another man. It grounds women squarely in the role of a possession, to be transferred from one family to another: from one man to another. It also tradition-ally sanctions sex within the institution of marriage where it can be safely contained. If women do not marry, whether through their own choice or not, there is no such symbolic separation, and fathers may continue to feel responsible for the welfare of their daughters. This was the case for my own father, who felt, whether or not I was living with a man, that because I did not marry I was still his little daughter who needed looking after. A daughter's age is irrelevant: from this viewpoint, no husband means no security. This is also Stanley's view on his daughter Rosemary, even though she had rejected the idea of marriage since her early teens. His strong moral views on sex meant that he could never properly accept Rosemary having such a relationship, nor living together with a man without being married. He described earlier the pain he felt when she lost her virginity, which in his eyes represented the loss of his control over her. The main reason he could not completely accept her pregnancy at the age of thirty-eight is because she is not married.

If marriage is the formal ceremony in which fathers 'give away' their daughters to the care and protection of another man, this should signify a separation, a letting go in their relationship and a relinquishing of paternal authority. Barbara is married with a baby daughter. Her father John is from a generation with strict moral views on sexuality, who even revealed to Barbara that he would have liked her husband to ask his permission to marry. Barbara describes how her father has tried to step back from his role since she has been married:

'I think when I got married it's like my father gave me away almost literally, I didn't realise it at the time, but I think if you are a close family it's not too stupid. And I think he made a conscious decision when we got married that that was it, he wouldn't interfere, so he can't tell us anything. Like I only realised it when he wanted to criticise my driving the other day. He led up to it and it took him half an hour, saying I know you're married and grown up . . . and it was something quite small. He wouldn't interfere if he thought he was interfering with Will.'

Furthermore, Barbara found that all the family sexual taboos had magically lifted and she was now treated like a sexual adult:

'Soon after I got married we slept in the same bed in his house. We lived with them for three months. That was very strange to me that I had lived with his rules, and sex under his roof was a definite No before. It felt very odd, I thought it was funny really. It was sort of expected of me, because that's what married people do! There was this very strong feeling that you don't, and then suddenly there's this strong feeling that you do! I'm sure he would have been very worried if we'd had single rooms!'

The subject of fathers, daughters and sexuality is a complicated one. It is one that clearly affects both sides of the relationship, but can more seriously influence daughters in their own present and future sexual lives. There are positive and negative aspects, but here I have concentrated on exploring some of the issues around fathers' attitudes within the family, their jealousy and possessiveness and related power and control over women. For many fathers, recognising the sexual potential of their daughters represents danger. They consequently avoid talking about sex within the family, and find it hard to relinquish their control and responsibility for their daughter and her sexuality to another man. This has been traditionally sanctioned through the formal institution of marriage. For their part, daughters find their father's attitudes towards virginity, sexuality and women's freedom in general to be often restrictive and irrational. Fathers do not or cannot articulate the complexities, which may not even be clear to themselves. Feelings may be translated into distance and transmitted as dogma. Sexuality is full of double standards. Society nods acknowledgement to women as separate, independent, sexual beings. In reality, girls and women are finding this hard to achieve, and the father–daughter relationship often provides a significant obstacle.

Chapter 5

Other men in her life

'I think father–daughter relationships affect your choice of partner, or whether you choose to have a partner. I think you do look for husbands with the same qualities as your father, or one with exact opposite qualities – what you've liked or not liked about him. I suppose more so when you're all girls, my father was really the only male [role] model.'

Barbara

'Certainly there are many elements in my father's personality which I have unwittingly looked for in my partner. That feeling of total dependability is very important to me, plus strength coupled with tenderness. Although my father has a lot of shortcomings as a partner, he has been an ace father.'

Sonia

'Do I choose ineffectual men like my father or is it that I choose men who will disappoint me like my father disappointed me? But what am I saying? Aren't all women disappointed by men?'

Shirley

It is no surprise that the relationships women have with their fathers exert a powerful influence on the sort of men they choose as their lovers and husbands, and the kinds of relationships they have with them. Usually the first man to feature prominently in their life, a father can set a precedent that women may want to pursue, or avoid. Even if fathers have been mainly absent from the family, they represent men and masculinity in a way that does not leave their daughters untouched. It may be thought that women look for men who show the qualities they admire in their fathers, and try to avoid those who have his most unlikeable characteristics, but this is far too simple. The men that women are attracted to may combine all sorts of qualities, and a woman may be attracted to different types of men at different points in her life. Fathers and daughters themselves have a complex relationship and a father may influence different parts of his daughter's personality, and this in turn can affect her reaction to the men she meets. They may spark off very differing responses and needs in her, so for instance, one man's personality may bring out her dependence and another her independence or her competitiveness. Different men may engage with different areas of her personality.

Many women's magazines regularly create questionnaires for readers to test if their partner is the right man for them. In a more serious vein, several authors in the United States have tried to grapple with this area. Recently, Secunda[1] differentiated types of fathers and daughters according to the nature of their relationship with the respective other. For each type of daughter suggestions are made as to the sort of man she will tend to be attracted to, and the likely outcome of these relationships. The testimonies and evidence are thought-provoking but there are inevitable problems in trying to define such distinct pathways. People are not so simply determined. In an earlier attempt to look at fathers and daughters in this way, Appleton,[2] a psychiatrist with a column in *Cosmopolitan* magazine at that time, is somewhat less neatly categorising. While drawing out the potential problems in the relationship, and the probable consequences for daughters, he also supports a human capacity for flexibility, recovery and change.

In the light of these approaches, I am not looking in this chapter to find consistencies where none exist but to explore how the fathers and daughters in this research saw the daughter's relationships with other men. I was not surprised to find that some paternal characteristics of fathers, or of daughters' relationships with their fathers, were repeated with their lovers and husbands and others were not. Like a kaleidoscope, each relationship falls into its own pattern according to the individuals concerned and the circumstances of their relationship, and this can change over time. Some daughters I talked to had spent some thought on the sort of partner they found attractive. They were conscious of either seeking men different in some specific way from their fathers, or looking to reproduce some of his positive aspects.

Others had become aware in retrospect that they might already have done this unconsciously. For example, Fiona was one daughter in her early thirties who had been contemplating this process. She has a partner and two young children. Her father David divorced her mother and remarried when Fiona was very young, and in Chapter 2 she has recalled their early relationship, with especially vivid memories of visiting his home and family with her older sisters when they all tried anxiously to please their father. Despite his absence through her life, David has been a very powerful person for Fiona and she finds herself drawn to men with some of the qualities she sees in him:

'Me and my dad, out of all the other children, we look very similar, and are quite similar in personality. I'm loathe to admit it but I'm attracted to men who are quite similar to him, who are powerful and charming.'

Fiona had recently thought more about her father's influence during a course she had taken:

'We had this woman from Relate come and she did a chart where she worked out how often it is that you pick a partner who in some way echoes your own parent relationship. When she said this I said "Oh, rubbish, you'll never find a comparison with my partner and my father." She said sometimes people prove such an opposite that it's almost the same, they try to do it on purpose. And she did it for everyone in the room, and they were gobsmacked. I found loads of comparisons with Ben (my partner). Sometimes I see Ben as being powerful to the children – although he's far more affectionate. It's almost as though I chose him because I knew he would be that sort of a father, as if I did it on purpose because he's very physical and affectionate, but he still expects them to do what he says, he doesn't give them that much leeway on being themselves. Occasionally I see that and it's horrible.'

Although Fiona may have been drawn to her partner because she saw and needed more affection than she got from her father, she now also sees aspects of her father in him that she likes less. These kinds of likenesses are not always instantly apparent and it may be, for example, that after the flush of early love, an adoring partner who appears unlike a daughter's dominating father reveals some remarkable similarities as time passes.

From his own perspective, Fiona's father David, cannot perceive much resemblance between himself and his daughter's partner, and comments:

'He doesn't ever have a side of gregarious frivolity, one of the boys, this sort of thing. He doesn't seem to be tremendously interested in anybody very much, so in that way he's not like me. . . . And I'm that much more worldly, she hasn't married a worldly person. In a way you could say that as far as she could see on the first thought of meeting him, he's very much the opposite of me. I don't know though, it's very hard to know what lives are like in somebody else's household.'

People are made up of a variety of characteristics and it is not hard to detect some similarities and differences. Richard (who left being a technical representative to take a history degree in his thirties, and features in several other chapters) and his daughter Sophie (now at university) have a positive father–daughter relationship that is featured frequently in this book, and have many shared interests and activities. One might expect Sophie to look for aspects of her father in her boyfriend Simon. She observes:

'In some respects Simon's like him, he's very generous. I think if it's true that we look for someone like our fathers, then I've looked for something like him, in that Simon is very caring, and he tends to take things seriously. My dad said when I was first going out with him that he liked him and he was also pleased from a father's point of view that he felt Simon was responsible and safe and he didn't worry about me. So I suppose in that respect they are alike, but not that similar, not to me anyway. Like his family's not at all academic, never read anything, never really watches TV. But since he's been living here, and obviously my dad reads the paper every day and watches the news and always talks about things, Simon has become a lot more aware I think, of politics and so on. Sometimes I hear my dad say something and a couple of says later I'll hear Simon say it to to his mum. It's quite strange but I think it's nice. . . . I think the main difference between Simon and dad is Simon much prefers being out getting his hands dirty. My dad would quite happily spend all day reading.'

For his part, Richard could not see many qualities that they shared, he saw their views and interests as being quite different, and Simon as being more practical and less academic, but as he commented, 'I suspect you'd have to go to a third or fourth party to get a clear view on this.'

Some girls grow up idolizing their fathers. This may stem from the close nature of their early relationship. She may be his favourite, and become 'daddy's girl'. Idolization can also take place from afar, as girls build up a fantasy image of their powerful fathers but are not able to have a close relationship with them. As children grow up, they usually develop a reasonably accurate appraisal of each other's qualities and faults, and idols become 'normal' people. There were a few daughters who spoke to me in glowing terms of their fathers. For them he represented someone who was (almost) perfect and could be relied on to do everything and sort anything out. Jean talked of growing up with this view of her father. She is twenty, a student living in Scotland who has five brothers and sisters. Her mother works at a special school and her father is now retired from his job as a foundry manager. Recently she has begun to see that her father is not faultless after all:

'He's the kind of person that if any of us are in any bother, the first person you go to is my dad. He'll sort it out for you. One thing I always say about my dad is that my dad can do anything, or if anything's broken he'll fix it. . . . But I think it was a difficult stage to go through, feeling that my dad was infallible. And then that time he was shouting at me I realised that he had handled the situation wrongly, and so he was not infallible. I had this image that my dad could fix anything, but as you get older you realise he's human.'

Whatever the nature of this paragon of a man, and whether he is constructed by the father or the daughter, this image can prove a tough one to maintain and an even harder example for any prospective boyfriend or husband to follow.

Another daughter whose father could do anything was Margaret. In other chapters she has described her closeness to her father Raymond, as well as her rebellion against him and her mother and the expectations of their Jewish family life on the outskirts of London. Amidst all the family turmoil, she has always considered that her father can do anything – at least anything practical, material and secure – and this is what she appreciates most in Keith, her second husband. Despite the many clashes when she was younger, Margaret was always his favourite daughter and he retained his insuperable qualities:

'My father can do anything! I still believe it – really! Practically as
well, he can do anything. He made their settee and armchairs, and
he made himself a suit just to see if he could do it. He carved an
Adam fireplace out of wood. . . . My father is wonderful! That's
what I want [from a man]. Keith's not such a perfectionist but in
my mind, come the end of the world I will be okay because I've
got Keith. He can make and do anything, and that's from my dad.
Keith's got his own business, like my dad. He is just like my dad,
he does what men are supposed to do. Keith also does what
women are supposed to do as well! He does all the cooking. He
cashes the child benefit, anything practical he'll just do it. Whether
he really can do everything, and whether my father can do it, I
still believe it, and it gives me enormous pleasure if we all get
together and my father and Keith go off and chat together about
making something, it's that shared practicality. My first husband
didn't do that, which was probably one of the reasons it wasn't
okay. . . . My father provided the material things of life. Although
he did go through a bad patch I was very protected from that. It
was a very secure relationship, I never doubted it.'

Margaret's father was around in the family throughout her
childhood and the admiration she feels for him is in the context of
his secure presence. Carole is a daughter who holds a great
admiration for her father even though he was absent for much
of her early childhood. Aged thirty-five and training to be a
counsellor, she wrote about her father and how she felt he
influenced her relationships with men. She is now divorced with a
teenage daughter and feels strongly that her father has exerted a
powerful effect, with significant consequences on her life:

'My father has had a great influence on me, I feel for the good.
Perhaps being my father it had an effect (probably strong) on who
I chose as a husband. I am now divorced! (as is my sister – we
married similar types of men). I feel that now, as I look back on
my marriage, perhaps having my father as he is will make it hard
for me to choose another partner. For whatever reasons I chose
my husband I now wonder about future choices. I feel that fathers
(like mothers) have a very strong influence on females' lives just
by existing. My father was absent a lot when I was under five . . .
but even being absent he was a powerful presence. He still calls
me baby and is a very caring, loving (though not physically) and
gentle man who will forgive repeatedly until pushed too far, hardly

ever loses his temper, and is funny, kind and an awfully hard act to follow! I would love to have a man similar to him. But I don't feel I'm in love with my father. I do like having him as a role model and am fascinated by the projections I used to put on my husband to make myself believe he was like my father! I'm stuck on anything negative to say about my father, perhaps a bit of pedestal-building here, and perhaps that is negative because of the way it affects my attitude to men.'

As Carole observes, her attitude to her father can get in the way of her accepting an apparently less 'perfect' man as a partner.

While some of the reasons why and the processes by which women choose their partners are unconscious, or may only be seen in retrospect, others involve a deliberate attempt to ensure that certain aspects of their potential relationships are quite different from that between their fathers and mothers. For example, Jane is a fifty-nine-year-old retired teacher who grew up with her parents and four brothers and sisters. Her father was a local-government official and her mother was a primary-school teacher until having children. After a warm and positive childhood relationship with her father, their relationship diverged somewhat (in common with that of several other women who wrote to me) due to strong differences in political attitudes. Because of this Jane became very critical of him in early adulthood, but looking back she believes he was a good father and grandfather to her own children, and the reservations she has are bound up with his treatment of her mother:

'He was the sort of man that found it much easier to blame than to praise. This was true to some extent in his relations with us children, but it was most obvious in the way he treated Mother. . . . Father blamed Mother for not being able to manage on her somewhat meagre housekeeping allowance: their rows about this were acrimonious and often left Mother in tears. I hated these upsets and always identified with Mother's point of view. I thought Father was mean. Later when I began to form serious relationships with men I wasn't quite sure what I was looking for in a permanent partner but I knew for certain that he had to be generous with his money.'

Jane reacted against her father's meanness with money, which is a fairly straightforward response. Other deeper facets that may be contained in close family relationships cannot be avoided so easily. For instance, women who have experienced some level of violence from their fathers may differ a lot in the ways they see male violence; the kinds of men they are attracted to as partners; and whether or not they are violent themselves. It is not a straightforward process and all situations and individuals are different. However, as was suggested in Chapter 3, there is some potential for a cycle of violence to develop by which children of violent parents tend to respond in similar family situations with violence themselves. It has also been suggested that women who have had violent fathers may be unconsciously attracted to men who have a similar tendency to be violent. Although some women do fall into a repeating involvement with violent men, this does not necessarily have to keep occurring. As Appleton[3] points out, daughters may move between various sorts of partners, and if one relationship has caused pain, they will look for a different sort of person. People are not necessarily locked into a fixed cycle. Becoming conscious of what has gone on in the relationship and the effects it has had can make people better able to avoid doing this again.

For example, Judy's violent relationship with her father has been described at length in Chapter 3. He was very violent with her (and her mother) throughout Judy's childhood in the north of England, and the pattern was repeated with her first husband. It was only after she left him and was totally removed from the situation that she could painfully examine what had happened and understand how and why it occurred. Judy met her first husband in her mid-teens: she became pregnant by him as a way of escaping from home and from her father. She recounts:

'I'd met this older man. I just thought all men were like my father. It was obvious how young I was – I was fifteen and I think he was about twenty-seven, and I looked young for my age. I didn't have any power, I just did what men, well, I did what my dad told me, and I think in many ways he was very much like my dad. He was domineering, very opinionated, very sexist, awful. When I was pregnant, he lived with me but he'd just go off and leave me and I was totally powerless again. I think I was looking for someone to take me away from my dad, protect me from my dad so it had to be someone big, someone tough, and it had to be someone older, because somone younger couldn't do it. In his own way he was very immature, very irresponsible, because I was a virgin. It took me a while to get out of that cycle of – well, not necessarily being attracted to – but looking to men like my dad with qualities of being tough and strong and big and dominant; and not having any respect for men who were quiet and gentle. They just weren't in my vocabulary, in my perception – God, they could never be regarded as men you know, if they could never fight, if they couldn't hit me.

In a very perverse way I came to accept it was normal for men to hit women, and if a man didn't look as if he could hit you then he wasn't a man. Other girls would only envy me with a man who was big and tall and strong and fighting. Thankfully I've changed! And I think I've only broken away from it because when the children were old enough to go to school I actually made the decision to go back and get myself educated, because I had no qualifications whatsoever, and my dad was very hostile to that . . . I think it was only then that I realised how ignorant he was: before that he'd always told us how clever he was.'

Rosemary and Stanley are another daughter and father whose violent clashes of will are described in Chapter 3. The nature of their conflictive relationship has not, however, necessarily meant that Rosemary sought out equally violent partners, but she did like them to have as much strength of will as herself. Now in her late thirties, and aware of these tendencies in herself, she observes that her present partner, Matthew, is more like the reverse of her father:

'I don't like people who aren't strong, well, yes and no, I'm not sure. I'm so used to doing battles that I can't stand it if people don't know how you do battle. I hate it if they're not happy with feelings, that's the good side of it all. Or they couldn't cry or whatever. If I've ever noticed that I was with them because they were like my dad I'd put an end to it. I've always been quite conscious of that. If anything I've wanted people who are gentle. I can't think of anyone who's been particularly like him. He's almost too present you see, to need a replacement substitute, he's quite large enough in my life anyway.

Matthew is very different to him. I think the thing that initially got Matthew and I together was understanding what it was like having grown up with (dominating) fathers like that. I don't think either of us had had relationships with people who really understood that, and how important it was to appreciate that it would still play itself out, and they needed to understand what was going on. And my dad thinks Matthew's wonderful: it's the first of my partners that I've taken to meet my dad that he's liked. He just sort of took to him, a complete contrast. But Matthew's really very nice you see, I suspect it's that he's not a threat.'

Her father Stanley confirmed her views:

'I like Matthew. I think he's a very stable chap. If he stays with Rosemary then I think she'll get on very well. I get on with him all right. . . . I wouldn't really know how strong a character he is as regards their personal relationship, but knowing Rosemary, if she makes up her mind not to get married she won't; on the other hand if she makes up her mind to get married he [Matthew] wouldn't stop her.'

Although Rosemary had not reproduced a violent relationship with Matthew, she was aware that she had taken on some of her father's bullying temperament and had tried to deal with it:

'If you've been treated with violence you do repeat it and it's just as easy for a woman to do it as for men. It has happened a couple of times with Matthew but he knows me well enough to know – you see, violence and fear are very close together. I think violence is about people being really terrified, and I've told Matthew the thing to do is just to move in on me. All I'm doing if I'm being like that is I'm desperate for somebody to really want me and love me, so even if I start hitting, to keep holding on, then I just burst into tears. These two are very very closely tied up. He knows me well enough to know that's what it is, but it actually hasn't happened for ages.'

If fathers are potentially so influential in their daughters' development, how far do they increase in importance if there are no other male role models around, such as when a girl is an only child, or one of several sisters with no brothers or close male relatives or friends? It could place a potentially heavy responsibility on a father for how his daughters view men and their expectations of them. For example, Maureen is thirty-two, divorced, and works as a temporary secretary in London. When she was young, her father's work as a patent agent took him away from their home in the south of England for much of the time. He later divorced her mother and married someone else, but remained a very important person in her life. In her teens she lived with her father after her mother had moved out of the family house and her two sisters had left home, until the time when her father's second wife moved in. Maureen writes about her father's role in her attitudes and expectations about men:

'He has played a big part in my development as any parent does by being or not being there, and by choice of education. My sisters and I were very shy and all went to all-girls schools, so what little we saw of him was the only male in our lives. It gave me a pretty distorted view! For all my father's faults he is/was intelligent and knowledgable. I thought all men were like him and was deeply shocked when I found out the horrible truth! I never forgave them. In retrospect I can see he influenced my choice of husband – there were a lot of similarities, but I had no qualms about emasculating my husband! I'm afraid I took out a lot of my anger on him (not that he didn't deserve it!) . . . it's clear that my disappointment in my father is reflected in my disappointment in men in general. I don't think my father's all that bad as men go, but since he forced me to face the fact that when it came down to it I'm utterly alone, I've decided it's a waste of time investing in a relationship that doesn't pay off. I'd rather live with the daily reality of being alone than be constantly disappointed. That makes me sound bitter and that I'm judging all men by my father, but I'm not. I've come across all sorts of men in all sorts of circumstances and I'm still not impressed.'

Maureen felt she was affected by being one of several daughters in an all-girl family. From the other side, men can be equally aware of the potential effects on daughters of them being the only male person in the family. One such father was John, now seventy with four grown-up daughters. His relationship with the youngest, Barbara, has been described in earlier chapters. He expressed his concern:

'I have a guilt complex about being the only male. I feel they've been deprived from knowing what to expect. I've monopolised the male aspect of their lives and all they expect is what I've shown them . . . that's what I regret, not even a brother to see what another man is like; and they went to girls' schools. I think they've been deprived of male company in their formative years.' His daughters are all married with children and John is also anxious that his example may have affected their choice of husbands: 'What worries me most is that they see the ideal husband for themselves in the good things in me. I feel very close to the eldest one, and her husband is modelled on me.' John has a very critical nature, and it seems no accident that his four daughters did not submit their potential husbands to his scrutiny before the relationships were well established. He comments: 'We never met a single boyfriend until we were told they were engaged. Boyfriends were brought back as a *fait accompli*, although they were living away from home anyway.'

Barbara was aware of her father's nature, and wanted him to approve of her choice of partner:

'I suppose in one way I looked for a husband that would please him and get on with him, but when it came to it I haven't had much feedback. In fact it's me that has to live with him, so in a way my parents are right not to interfere with us, and they get on well with him. Will is like my dad, he's got a lot of interests and really likes learning. In general he's interested in politics. I suppose he's similar in his views on things. It's hard to say what attracted me to Will in the first place. He is less critical but I don't know if I noticed that or not.'

When asked what sort of man they want for their daughter, parents often say they just want their daughters to be happy with whatever man they choose to be with. This, however, may be a little too simple, especially where fathers are concerned, who are often rather particular about what they want (or don't want) for their daughters. Barbara observes about her father John:

'I think there was always a sense of "Nobody's quite good enough for my little girls." When I brought Will back and said I was going to get married, they were terribly surprised, Dad nearly threw his tea over the carpet. I think they were pleased. But as I say, there was this feeling coming through that he probably wasn't good enough for me. In the beginning there was a bit of tension between my dad and Will. I think that sort of drifted away. I'm not quite sure when it was, probably something to do with when I had the baby, then they had something in common. I suddenly turned round to Will one day and said "You and dad get on okay now", but I never overtly said anything.' It may be, as Barbara implies, that being a grandfather had demonstrated something that John shared with his son-in-law and somehow placed their relationship on a different and more equal footing.

The sentiment that 'No-one is good enough for my daughter' is a familiar one. It was one that was described by David, a London journalist now in his sixties, and the father of Fiona, who was quoted earlier in the chapter. He articulates the contradictions and resentment that men can feel when another man takes the top position in their daughter's life:

'I think the truth is, to a father no man is right for his daughter. On the other hand, any man that she wants is right, so it's quite a strain in a way I find. But that feeling when you look, there's your daughter, who you have quite strong feelings for and you feel to some extent you look out at the world through her eyes, or perhaps you hope she looks out at the world through your eyes. . . . And suddenly this man appears, and you look at him, and just his face can sort of give you a pain, you know. You think "How can you? – Are you going to wake up every morning looking at that nose, and his eyes, his eyebrows, and that awful way of clearing his throat!" You can make a whole list of things. You see your daughter looking at him like that and you think, in her eyes here's this marvellous creature. She must be mad! But she's in love . . .'

What is more, she has also fallen for someone who is usually a lot younger than her father, and this may strike another jealous chord. David continues:

'Of course he's younger than you, thirty years younger than you are. And she says "He's got this – whatever it is – let him tell you about it." And you listen and you think "Oh God, I've heard that a hundred times, there's nothing new in that." Is she really so impressed by something like that, just because this spotty person tells her. So it is a mystery.'

Fathers want the best for their daughters, and this includes a man who will not take advantage of her sexually or any other way. Hence they often profess to want their daughters to find someone who is steady, responsible and safe. This may be a contrast to the way they see themselves as being when they were younger, so there may exist a contradiction between identifying with a boyfriend who is a bit wild, but not really wanting him near their daughter. Earlier in the chapter Sophie, Richard's nineteen-year-old daughter, spoke of the similarities and differences between her father and her steady boyfriend Simon. Richard himself can see few resemblances, and expresses paternal relief that Simon is not as irresponsible as he was at an earlier age:

'I don't see many of my qualities in Simon, but I really couldn't say . . . she's always shown an inclination towards what I can only describe as rather likeable tearaways. Now Simon isn't really that style. Perhaps what Sophie sees is something I don't necessarily see, but is a common factor to all of them. And for all I know there may be some factor in him that's also in me, but I couldn't see what it is . . . quite frankly, if she had met me at his age – I think probably she's better off with him than she would have been with me at that age. I think I was more of a liability than he is. I think he's more moral than I would have been sexually, but that's for different reasons. I think he is more likely to be faithful to her than I would have been. So it's swings and roundabouts.' Richard identifies with the 'tearaways' but wants a safe and secure partner for his daughter.

In order to develop their own personal and sexual identities, it is necessary for daughters to separate themselves from their fathers. No matter how devoted a father and daughter may be, it is as important for them to respect each other and give each other space as it is in any other close relationship. For a girl to develop into an autonomous individual, this is especially important. This will be facilitated too by her father's interest and encouragement and his praise and support, which can help to fuel her own aspirations and achievements. This is not always easy to do: families have complex structures and interactions, and there are inevitable clashes between parents and children, especially in the years of adolescence when children are forming identities of their own. The role of fathers in this process is complicated by the issue of sexuality, as we have seen in Chapter 4, and a man who tries to stop his 'little girl' from growing up can damage his daughter's ability to develop a strong and independent sense of herself, with the confidence to go for what she wants. If a father prepares his daughter for the adult world, she will also be able to handle relationships with men better and be able to tolerate their weaknesses and enjoy their strengths. Not expecting too much she will be less likely to be constantly disappointed, but by not settling for too little she will not be taken advantage of and will be able to allow a man close enough to enjoy their relationship.

In this context, some women find it difficult to develop an

independent sense of self. For those who are deeply bound up with their fathers, it can be extremely hard to free themselves from this. For example, Anne is thirty-one, single and is currently doing advocacy work. She was brought up more like an only child because the four children her father had with his first wife had all left home by the time she was a few years old. She has always had a very intense relationship with her father, who did shiftwork as a fireman. They did many things together when she was young, from which her mother was largely excluded. The relationship betwen Anne and her mother was strained and hostile and that between her parents often violent. To some extent Anne took her mother's place with her father and he did not want to let her go her own way. Boyfriends were therefore definitely not welcomed, and got short shrift from Anne's father, as she describes:

'He only ever met one of my blokes, and he hated him, and he gave him a really hard time. He had a go at him when he was in our house and he knew he couldn't really retaliate. What he was looking for was for my bloke to say "Sod off!" and it would've been fine, but because he didn't square up to him he was contemptuous and it was hopeless then. It's almost like a ritual dance, and it affected my view of him, I thought he was a weed as well. . . . But my dad made his life a misery and of course that had a knock-on effect for me, and this bloke hated my dad. . . . It would be hard for dad to accept a man in my life. He'd like it if it was someone from a job that he approved of . . . and if it was someone like him it would probably be okay. If there's ever a hint I've been out with anyone foreign he goes up the wall. It really hurts my feelings, it's so painful.' Anne reflects: 'I think he really held on to me emotionally, and I can understand that. He hasn't made it easy for me any way along the line. He begged me not to leave home [at eighteen], really didn't want me to leave. I think now, looking back, I just haven't separated from my dad at all. I think I'm only just getting to that point, and I think it's affected my relationships with men a lot, I've had very low expectations. . . . Now I'll look for something more and something different from my dad. My dad's very much like a man's man. He's very set in what he thinks are women's roles and men's roles. That isn't what I want for my life at all.'

If men express extreme attitudes and behaviour towards their daughter's sexuality, this can clearly cause many psychological problems in their future relationships. This was illustrated in the situation of Kate, who tells (in Chapter 4) how her father withdrew and rejected her as soon as she reached the stage of having boyfriends. Kate left school at fifteen to become a hairdresser, but later took a business studies course and does secretarial work in London. Now twenty-eight, it is only through therapy that she has been able to get a clearer perspective on that period of her life. She describes what happened:

'Our first major problem was when I took an interest in boys. I was fairly young – about thirteen – but completely innocent and a fairly normal and healthy girl. My parents had bought a newsagent's business the year before and worked seven days a week. . . . We saw little of our parents and the family atmosphere was tense. Dad wouldn't allow me to go out with boys and began to behave as if he hated me. Mum encouraged me to just get on with what I wanted to do (within reason) in an effort to keep the peace. Dad and I became completely isolated from each other and communicated via mum. There was strain all round but we never managed to talk about it. I spent most of my teenage years hating my dad because he was so hard, and couldn't stand the sight of me, he also took out any anger for me on my mum as well.

'Dad does not show any aspect of his sexuality apart from being a man's man, i.e. darts, horses and going to the pub for a drink. I now have major problems feeling comfortable with my own sexual desires. I've been off sex for about two years and can't get to the bottom of why. Sex seems okay for me when I'm not very involved with someone but when I need to expose an inner self it doesn't seem to be there. I feel blocked off, almost too ashamed of myself to even admit to myself what I feel and want to share with a man. I am sure that some of this goes back to that sudden change in how dad and I got on once I started to develop as a woman. This may sound crazy but the thought of having a child is very difficult because I still play down my sexual development with dad, so how can I manage a baby?'

Kate went to therapy to help her in her own personal relationships and found that her relationship with her father cropped up very frequently:

'Therapy helped me a good deal, I'd gone because I was feeling very uncomfortable within my relationship with my boyfriend. I thought I was frigid because sex felt awful. The therapist kept taking me back to my family and ultimately to dad. One very important thing we came across was how confused and hurt I felt over his rejection of me and how he behaved as though he really disliked me. This was very painful for me and I had buried this very deeply.'

Many unhappy childhood experiences may get suppressed deep inside the unconscious self, because they are too painful to carry around, but they have very significant effects on our lives and subsequent relationships, as Kate illustrates. Several other women who wrote to me had similarly discovered in therapy that their relationship with their father was crucially important in problems they had experienced in social and sexual relationships with men. Both Kate and her sister have suffered from anorexia nervosa, a condition usually involving strict dieting, exercise and use of laxatives to get rid of food. If it goes on for a long time it can have serious and sometimes fatal consequences. A significant number of young women suffer from it and it has often been found to be related to problems within family relationships.[4]

For many women now in their thirties and forties, there has been more contrast between their lives and those of their mothers than there is between present generations. There is a striking difference between the image and ideology of women's role before and after the Second World War. Before the war it was only working-class women and women in professions who were seen to have a legitimate reason to work outside the home. When women embarked on married life in the pre-war period, women's place was still seen as primarily in the home, caring for husband and family and largely dependent on the wages of their husbands. But for those girls born in the 1940s and 1950s, the outlook for women's education and careers was already changing a lot. Girls growing up at this time were gradually becoming aware and critical of the contradictions this produced in women's lives. Many of them, like myself, could see the difference between the lives and outlook of their mothers, who had stayed at home looking after their husbands and children, and the wider opportunities they were being encouraged to take up through education and changing ideas about women's role in society.

In this historical context, women from this generation may recognise that there are not just characteristics in their fathers that they wish to avoid in potential husbands or lovers, but it is also their parents' domestic relationship that they do not want to reproduce. Many such women want more than the marriage and childcare that had totally occupied many of their mothers' lives.

For example, Elaine was born in the mid-1940s and grew up in a working-class family in the west of England where her father worked on the railways and her mother always stayed at home to look after her and her two sisters. Both parents wanted their children to take full advantage of the post-war opportunities in education that they never had. Elaine in fact left school and became a secretary, but after some time working abroad she returned to train at art school and has pursued an artistic career ever since. Relationships with men have always taken a subordinate role in her life. She recalls her attitudes at school:

'I was always first, second or third at school. I didn't have a very high opinion of boys, and I could see from other girls that you got yourself pregnant and ended up staying in that country town and I knew I wanted to get away and for me it was the stupid ones that got trapped and that wasn't going to happen to me . . . I was probably quite sort of snotty. I wanted something better . . . I'm not sure if my decision not to marry (or lack of interest in marriage) is to do with my mother being at home full-time or to do with my father. I think on reflection it has more to do with the restrictions or constraints marriage would put on me, and men not coming up to my expectations, – now that could have to do with my father!'

Another member of this generation is Rosemary, quoted earlier, who is a few years younger than Elaine. She decided her views on marriage early in her life, and she sees these as at least partly influenced by her mother's marriage to her father Stanley, in which he dominated her mother in the same way he tried to dominate his daughter:

'When I was about thirteen or fourteen I told them I wasn't going to get married, it just seemed a ridiculous thing to do. I'd already been a bridesmaid to three cousins and one of them was divorced and the last thing I wanted to do was to be tied to somebody like my dad forever and not get away from them. I wasn't going to be beholden to someone like that thank you, I'd seen what he did to my mum. I was always very independent, I always knew my own mind. I don't think it was ever just in relation to him and being defiant about it, I think I actually did know what I wanted. I had a very strong sense of who I was.'

Both these daughters, Elaine and Rosemary, have very independent personalities and this characteristic in women is one that

Elaine believes many men find off-putting. She comments: 'My relationships with men are a series of disasters – they see me coming! Being quite independent and quite strong and powerful, it seems quite threatening to them.' Speaking on a similar theme, twenty-six-year-old Louise, an art and drama graduate working in a London office, has also developed a strongly independent identity, but more through the absence rather than the presence of her father. When her father left her mother ten years previously, she rejected him and identified strongly with her mother. She recalls him as always being somewhat detached from herself and the family, so she feels that she did not lose a very intense relationship. They did not see one another for several years, although he maintained contact with her younger brother. More recently, they have started rebuilding their relationship. The experiences of her teenage years have, however, had far-reaching effects on her personality and identity, and like Elaine, she believes that women with strong personalities frighten away prospective boyfriends:

'I saw [my mother] having to be ever so independent, having to work, having to bring in the money which wasn't easy, and run everything and do things she hadn't done before, like all the finances. Having seen her go through that, I've become very fiercely independent which I don't think helps in my relationships at all. I think men are just petrified of it, but there's nothing I can do about it. . . . It also affected my relationships in that I wanted a place of my own, and to live my own life.'

The issue of how and why men are 'petrified' of very independent women is a subject that needs to be explored separately. It reflects men's need to have power over women and their own insecurities and is likely to involve the general nature of the relationship between mothers and sons.

As a lesbian, Lesley intentionally rejects relationships with men, and her family situation has been described in more detail in the last chapter. It was about twenty years ago, in her late thirties, that she turned from men to women. She grew up having a close relationship with her father Bob, but moved closer to her mother in her teens. An only child, she always felt distant from the boyfriends she had at this time:

'I was in relationships most of the time but I just couldn't get close to them at all. There was always something more important to them, like the car, or football, or work, so I moved on. . . . My dad is very stereotypical as far as I'm concerned. He just represents everything I dislike about men, although I do like the qualities he has – he's generous to a fault and he's very kind, he would do anything for anybody. It's just what goes on in his head that worries me. I value the practical things because that's the only thing I can actually get together with him on. Other things we end up disagreeing on.'

Nevertheless, Lesley and her parents are mutually supportive: they are in regular contact and she has no reservations concerning talking about her sexuality with them or bringing lovers to visit. As discussed in the previous chapter, in many ways it may be easier for Bob to accommodate another woman in the family, than the potential competition represented by a boyfriend or son-in-law, who would almost certainly remove Lesley from needing his protection and help.

The ways that a father can influence his daughter's choice of men and the relationships they have with men is complex, but clearly has consequences that reach into many areas of her adult life. Girls' expectations from men, and the social and sexual patterns of their relationships with men, originate within the family through girls' experiences with fathers and brothers. They may then be transferred on to new relationships, but the manner in which this happens is not straightforward. Although it is possible to chart simple trends by which women consciously or unconsciously repeat or avoid characteristics in potential husbands and lovers that they have encountered in their fathers, this can vary between and within women's lives and choices of men. It does seem, however, that where fathers and daughters have given each other enough personal space and mutual respect this enhances their relationship with each other, and makes it easier for daughters to develop self-confidence, independence and an understanding of their own self-identity. Armed with these attributes, a woman may be able to perceive more clearly what they want from a potential lover or husband, and be more assertive within the relationship.

From the other side of the relationship, there are ways in which the man that a daughter brings into the family can affect her father. He may provide her father with an ally; on the other hand, a father may, for instance, feel overtaken in his role to protect his daughter, threatened by the relative youthfulness of her partner, or in competition with his physical and intellectual abilities. But a woman's husband or lover is not merely a substitute for her father as the male figure in her life, even if it is he who feels replaced. In today's society, in which marriage is not secure and women want more equal roles, the characteristics involved in the inter-relationships between fathers, daughters and the men in her life are fascinating, but very difficult to untangle.

Chapter 6

Ways of fathering

'A good father–daughter relationship is being really open and not the traditionally Victorian distant father, and being approachable. To be honest and to talk to your kids as if you want to talk to them, not as if they're a problem and they just get in the way, to give a child a really loving, caring background.'

Helen

'My mum would be doing the meals and washing up, my dad would tend to watch TV with me and play with me. In a way I think I thought of him more as a friend, almost like a brother I didn't have, and my mum was more of a parent. My dad sometimes would be a parent as well.'

Sophie

'It's a good relationship. I like his humour; he cheers me up from feeling bored. . . . If I was in a really bad mood I'd probably say all sorts of little touchy things. If he's wound me up, I could really yell about it. When I'm in a calm mood, well, he just exists, he's my dad, he's just there.'

Laura

What makes a good father–daughter relationship? Are such relationships affected by the structure of the family? What are the experiences of lone fathers and daughters living together? And those of fathers who are trying to become like a 'real' father to daughters who are not their own? This chapter outlines some of the characteristics that have been assigned (especially by women) to definitions of a 'good' father–daughter relationship, and explores some specific experiences of fathers and daughters in situations other than the so-called nuclear family.

Sophie and Richard (whose relationship has already been well documented) consider theirs is a good relationship. Richard has concentrated his fathering on Sophie, his only child, aged nineteen, and has given the process much thought:

'If there's been any plan it's been to expose her to as many experiences as possible. Wherever I could I shared whatever I had with her. Perhaps I could see a long-term return to me, in that later she could share things with me. . . . To some extent what's happened now is what I was really looking forward to, someone that I could talk to and who would bring back ideas to me. I've always had a great deal of pleasure from her company. I suppose I have done very well out of the relationship and I just hope I have made the effort to make some input for her benefit. Hopefully it's been good for her. . . . I think she would hesitate to hurt me by making a decision that she knew I would be upset about. I think her affections for me are secure, but I think as she is meeting more people my place in the academic or intellectual order is slipping. I think we're reaching a normal adult relationship. I would still assume to give her advice in a way she wouldn't give me, I suppose the fact that I am her father, one still continues to assume that one can give advice, and she's sufficiently courteous to listen to it.'

For her part, Sophie observed:

'I think we have got a good relationship and I think it's mainly because he's never tried to make me do anything or forced me into anything. Probably tolerance is the most important thing, and always talking to each other, you don't let problems build up. . . . I've had a very stable family. I think I've always felt, no matter what else is happening I've always got my parents.'

This sense of mutual affection, respect and tolerance has enabled Sophie to pursue her own life taking her father's unconditional love, interest and support for granted. In contrast to this, Anne's intense relationship has been characterised by her father's extreme dependency on her. She was the only child of her mother, while having four step-brothers and sisters from her father's first wife who had left home when she was young. The closeness of Anne and her father alienated her mother and reinforced the inter-dependency between Anne and her father. It is only recently that she has been able to try to work through these issues:

'I know myself and I take it for granted how much I love my dad. But I feel my dad's love has always been very conditional on some level. That doesn't help you move on, it doesn't help you be brave. I felt that I lived my young life fighting, now I don't need to do that, and I now feel much more loved by my friends, I've redefined my emotional life. I think a good father–daughter relationship is the things I haven't had – things like unconditional love.'

Tolerance and unconditional love go hand in hand with an acceptance of people on their own terms, and this can apply equally to parent–child relationships. In this respect Margaret, whose Jewish family upbringing and rebellion has been described earlier, strongly agrees:

'A father should be accepting of the child on her terms and value what she's doing on her terms. That's what I think makes a good father–daughter relationship. I believe it's down to the parents – the father needs to be understanding. I think daughters do think about their relationships with their fathers and they do the emotional work. My dad is not at ease and happy with emotions. It's extra difficult for fathers to do that. But if they can do that, then that's what makes the relationship. I would say I had a good father–daughter relationship.'

The response and interest from women in participating in this research confirms that daughters put in a lot more emotional work than their fathers in their relationships with one another. One father said:

'A good father–daughter relationship is that either one can go to the other and pour out their heart to them honestly. That's the perfect relationship. I'm quite sure she could come to us and say anything and if needs be I can say anything to her.'

This is easier to say than to do, and this father also implies that the emotional initiative is more likely to come from his daughter.

Many daughters stressed the importance of verbal communication with their fathers. Jean, for instance, is a twenty-year-old university student living in Scotland. Her father was a foundry manager, now semi-retired, who is mainly at home while Jean's mother is out at work. This arrangement has given Jean more opportunity to talk with her father:

I don't feel close since I left school. In lots of ways he's not shown an interest in what I'm doing, particularly when I started college and in the work I'm doing now. I just feel that if he really cared for me he'd be interested in that. I felt hurt when I realised it, but now I'm used to it. But then again, it's not that he doesn't care; he certainly cares about me, he bought me the car when I moved here for instance. But I suppose for me, he doesn't care in the right areas, and there isn't a lot I can do to change that. . . . So it's mum I go to, I talk to mum, and now of course, dad says, "I'll leave you two to it. You've got a lot to catch up on." And he says it in a real hurt way. And I think, "God, it's nobody's fault. He's just not interested in what I'm doing." Mum is, so mum and I just sit for hours and hours. It seems a shame I can't have that relationship with my dad. I suppose he thinks we have a good relationship in some ways. I know some relationships where they don't speak to one another, it's just superficial, so I suppose we do go a bit deeper than that, we do have discussions and arguments.'

Her father Bob, is apparently unaware of her feelings and he takes a more positive view of their relationship:

'I always say I've got more things in common with Lesley, like I'm interested in bird watching and we've got an interest in camping, and cars, because she's mechanically-minded, we do things together on her car. Generally speaking, Lesley and her mother have got things that interest women in common. In some things they're more involved, they go out shopping together and get on well in that respect. I tend to talk to her more to advise her. I'm pleased we've both got a good relationship. She still tends to ring us at home if she's got a problem. . . . We can talk pretty easily. I can't think of many things we can't talk of if it comes to sex and things like that . . . and we discuss politics quite a bit. If I talk about feminism I've got to be very careful, I get accused of being chauvinistic. It's a job to say if her relationship with her mother is stronger, she's probably spent more time with her mother. We discuss things, we have semi-arguments, her mother gets a bit upset because we get quite het up. I quite enjoy it, giving different points of view, from that respect we get on well.'

For Lesley, her father's political attitudes have been part of the reason she feels that their relationship has changed. Her feminist and anti-racist views conflict with those of her father. Radical political differences were described by several other daughters as being a source of distance and conflict between them and their fathers. While Bob thinks these are just issues he and Lesley get heated about, for his daughter, they have created a more significant gulf. She comments:

'For us to have a good father–daughter relationship we'd have to change the politics. When we talk about women's issues and things, he listens but he doesn't really hear what I'm saying. He sees it from his side all the time. In some ways I wonder if I respect my dad. . . . I feel sorry for him because we haven't got the relationship that he thought we could. I suppose when I was a kid that was fine, when I was going through my tomboy era. I suppose what would have been different is if they'd had an equal say in my upbringing, because I know they differed and mum got her way. Mum was the major force in bringing me up; she's always been the dominant one of the two in my life, and still is.'

If love, tolerance, acceptance and communication are a central part of the formula given by daughters for a good father–daughter relationship, then these probably apply similarly for a good father–son (or indeed any other) relationship. It would be interesting to explore whether sons put the same emphasis on affection and communication.

Much is taken for granted in family relationships, while at the same time the negotiation of certain issues can be like treading on eggshells. If communication is difficult in a situation where a father lives with the family, it will obviously be even harder in one where he is predominately absent. In the past, the effects of father absence on children, mainly boys, received a lot more attention from psychologists than the impact of their presence.[1] Fathers can be absent from family life for reasons such as work demands, divorce, separation and death. If a father dies when his children are young, the empty space this creates may be carried on into adulthood. For instance, one woman wrote:

'I have read many books about the mother–daughter relationship but have always felt that my relationship with my father has had a much greater influence in my life. My father died when I was thirteen years old. I am now thirty-eight and every day of my life is affected by both his absence and his presence. Not having a father around during my teenage years (or any adult male model) has, I feel, affected my relationships with men ever since.'

I received a significant number of letters like this from women who believed that the loss or absence of their father earlier in life had had permanent effects, and several other researchers have looked at the situation of daughters without fathers[2] and how this may have affected them.

The effects on children of 'losing' their father in some way depend on various factors, including: the nature of the absence; the age of the children; what kind of father–child relationship had already developed; the way the separation occurred; and how the relationship subsequently develops. It is not easy to make generalisations: children may have various reactions. For instance, they may create an idealised image of their father which omits his faults and the mundanities and conflicts of everyday life; they may perpetually try to please him; they may constantly resent his disappearance from their day-to-day life; or a combination of all of these.

SEPARATED FATHER AND DAUGHTER RELATIONSHIPS

Many children live in families from which their natural father is absent for a diversity of reasons. In the light of the increased divorce and separation rates, I am going to concentrate here on describing just two such illustrations. In both of these the father had moved away from the family home leaving the children in the care of their mother. The contact between a separated father and his children may vary widely from frequent and regular care to occasional holidays, and the quality of time spent together can also be variable. It is easy to assume there will be negative effects on children and the two illustrations here do, in fact, demonstrate some of these. Yet fathers can – and many do – maintain a positive relationship with their children, even though they no longer live together. It can, however, be a situation full of potential pitfalls and misunderstandings.

The first illustration is provided by Fiona and David, aspects of whose relationship appear throughout this book. Fiona's father David had left her mother when Fiona was small and although she and her two sisters were regular visitors to his new homes and families, she has already described how left out and dissatisfied she felt with his lack of closeness and affection, and how angry this still makes her feel:

'There's something very sticky about my relationship with him, I'm angry about the way he is. But I don't think I was able to be angry with my father ever, even as a child. . . . I worked out a few years ago that I was carrying this anger towards him around which I think was really my mum's. . . . I used to have a thing for ages that I was adopted, and also if I'd been a boy, he wouldn't have gone . . . but I think even if my mum had still been married to him, he would have been quite distant, I think that's the way he is with children. But I always thought he wasn't the father I wanted him to be. I wanted him to be much more affectionate, much more physical, although he is quite a physical man and he seems to get women going. But nothing was quite good enough for him: he wanted us – all of us, not just me – to be more interesting, more outgoing.'

Fiona has never been able to tell her father how she feels because she assumes he would never admit it and tell her he was sorry: 'I think he'd say "Oh darling, how could you be so wrong, of course I've always loved you", and that doesn't help either. I want him to say "Oh, God, did I? Oh, no." I want him to say "I didn't mean to", and I want him to realise that what I'm saying is real for me. But I think he'd dismiss it a bit like "Oh, you were young, you didn't realise."'

We can never assume that if David and Fiona had remained together in the same family that their expression of love and communication would necessarily have been significantly different. But when people who take a significant role in our lives go absent, their apparent power to withdraw from our lives can exert a very strong effect. Fiona comments:

'I think being a father was a sideline for him, maybe he never had a chance really to carry it through. It would have been interesting if he'd been with one set of children their whole life, maybe he would have been different. That's my thing, I think basically I don't know if he really loved me. He would say it, and whenever he phones he says, "Bye then, I love you" and it makes me cringe. It's like, no, you can't start loving me now. . . . Part of me thinks he must be quite insecure. He loves his children because they're extensions of him, and he likes people who can do things that he can understand. Maybe he wasn't confident as a father, he was going through these splitting-ups and felt very guilty about it. He'll probably tell you "They're very important to me" and you'll think

"What's gone wrong here? A real breakdown in communication."
Obviously, he'll have a totally different slant on it, and in a way
you'll think what he believes is more correct, because he's an adult
and he can remember time gaps and things, whereas as a child you
don't really. I think he thinks he loves us but I still think he didn't
give me what I wanted. I want someone who just thinks everything
you do is wonderful. I'm sure my father never looked at me
running around as a child and thought "Isn't she wonderful?" He
was always too busy having his friends round. Whenever I talk
about it I always end up thinking, "God, I'm paranoid, this poor
little girl who wasn't loved." But I must have got it from
somewhere, and I don't feel that with my mum.'

Because Fiona wants David's approval, she feels she cannot risk
exposing herself to him in certain moods. Asking him for general
advice is fine, but if she is feeling really low she feels she would not
be presenting the right image. She cannot present herself as
vulnerable:

'I would go to him for advice, and I've gone to him in the past for
financial help. But it's like selected advice, some things I wouldn't.
I have to be wanting a good moan, but feeling quite eloquent or
whatever so I can always joke about it. I can go when I'm
depressed but funny, but if I'm feeling like stripped to me, I can't.
I can't rely on him to say "You're all right" sort of thing. And I can't
imagine him coming to me for advice, although I'd love him to.'

For his part, David is aware that all has not been well on his
daughter's side of their relationship:

'I think to some extent she slightly felt she was the neglected one.
I imagine if you're thinking that you've been neglected then you
think you're owed something. I sometimes feel that with Fiona I
have a very warm feeling because she's such an outgoing jolly
person. She's much less conventional than her sisters. She's got
the streak of the rebel.'

David also confirmed that he believed that fathers should not be
too close to their children: that if fathers are not around so much
this helps to stop them being placed on some kind of pedestal. In
his opinion he has provided sufficient closeness for his daughters:

'The girls came for two days every weekend and in the summer
we went off for a month camping around Europe, so I felt I

provided a closeness. On the other hand, my belief is that though you do have this connection with your children that makes them different from other people, you should let that go as naturally as possible. . . . I would say that they must take their own way. We all have our lives. They only have one father, I have five children. I have to divide it up. . . . I think Fiona probably feels she hasn't had as much continual affection and interest from me as she would like. I'm sorry about that but it's too late now. She's thinking of a sort of ideal time when she was growing up and I should have been there. I'm sorry that I wasn't. But this is all life, isn't it? What one must get out of one's head is that there is a plan to life.'

David is aware of the need to separate, but his creation of distance has served to promote dependency in the form of Fiona's need for approval, rather than the self-confidence he intended. He continues:

'I'd have been happy with two daughters and it would have made life easier. But then having two wives and each wants children you can't turn round and say "I don't think it's right – I've replaced myself and that's enough." But what am I doing adding five children to the world? On the other hand, if I'd had two daughters and I'd seen a lot of them I might have really mucked up their lives. Possibly I may have made it so that they couldn't find a man to match up, they might not have seen that man if my personality had been so heavy on two of them, but when it's spread it's better. Every advantage has got a disadvantage hasn't it?'

David is very philosophical and almost offhand about his relationship with his children, which has left Fiona with a sense of permanent dissatisfaction and a residue of anger. His distance is equivalent to a form of physical absence. In spite of seeing Fiona at regular intervals he has not been able to give her the assurance of paternal love that she needed. It is clearly still an important issue for her in their relationship.

There are other responses to fathers who leave the family. It depends on various factors, including the age of the child and the reasons for leaving. It can, for instance, create independence instead of dependence. In contrast to Fiona, anger and resentment were twenty-six-year-old Louise's reaction when her father Ian walked out on her and her mother and brother for another relationship. She was then sixteen. Consequently, she and her father have become very estranged. Louise rejected him and sided with her mother, who was devastated by the break-up of her marriage. Ian continued to have some contact with his son James, but not with Louise, and they did not see one another for four years from when she was seventeen. Ian recalls:

'I'd met somebody else and was leaving to be with her at some point in time, it wasn't through wanting to leave the family. . . . It was quite heartbreaking and very hard to do. When I was totally engrossed in the new relationship I was cut off from the children, I hardly saw Louise at all and she naturally became rather bitter. She really felt she wanted to support her mum, while James shrugged his shoulders and got on with things. . . . During this time I hardly saw either of them. It was a great gap in my life but something I couldn't do much about and I thought if I drifted in and out of their lives it would be disruptive. I thought they'd be better on their own for a while, and eventually things turned round and I did see them on a more regular basis.'

Fathers in this situation tend to maintain more contact with sons than with daughters. Ian's description of his son's reaction also suggests James may be distancing himself from his own emotions and feelings.

For the last couple of years Louise and Ian have been in contact and are slowly getting to know one another again. Louise cannot remember much about their relationship before he left. When she was fifteen they had started to get closer through playing tennis and jogging together. She recalls:

'In a way I don't think my father was involved in family life enough and my mother didn't involve him, it was a two-way thing. So when he opted out I didn't miss the family involvement. . . . I was aware that he wasn't with us really in his head. I felt almost he was looking in at me from the outside sometimes. . . . When he left I was pretty devastated but I could see my mother completely and utterly torn apart and that meant I felt my priorities lay with her, so I think I shut off from him completely. . . . When he went, somebody said to me I looked like my father and I stood in front of the mirror with a razor, I wanted to slash my face. I just felt I don't want to look like him. I couldn't forgive him for what he was doing to my mother and I think there's always a bit of it which says that if I had anything to do with him I was being disloyal to her. I don't think he could ever be what I would term as a normal father to me again because of that, and because we've missed those years. But I always knew that I'd have to see him again at some stage.'

Because of her father's absence in her life for these years, Louise feels as though they have now developed a more formal relationship which lacks the sense of mutual responsibility common to many parent–child relationships:

'I don't consider he's protective towards me like my mother is. On the whole I chat with my father about things and it's like talking to a friend rather than a father. I wouldn't say it was paternal, it's different. Having said that, if he were patriarchal towards me I think I'd throw it back in his face, he no longer qualifies for that role. I've often thought "You forfeited your right", but that doesn't mean to say we can't have a relationship on a different level. I've got to the stage with him where he takes me as I am and if he's not prepared to accept me as I am – tough – he doesn't take me at all. When I was fifteen I felt a lot of admiration for him, then what I felt when I wasn't speaking to him was that I had no respect for him whatsoever. I felt he had to earn his respect again from me. I wouldn't say I loved him, but I feel he's gaining respect in my eyes which he certainly didn't have for a long time. I think my father owes me, he's got to make an effort. If you've missed out on a period of someone's life you can never get that back. It's pointless trying to fill it in, you just have to start again. . . . If he wasn't my father he wouldn't be a man I would know, but I feel I should make the effort. I know that I would miss out and he would miss out.'

For Louise it has been more than the physical absence of her father that has changed their relationship. It is a product of the relative lack of closeness between them before he left, together with the manner in which he left and the consequences for her mother. Louise also finds it hard to accept her father at a physical level because he left her mother for someone else:

'I'm a very physical person, I like to hug people, but I don't feel physical towards my father at all. And that could go back to the fact that I thought there's something about him physically that has repelled me in the past and perhaps still does and that's because he was unfaithful to my mother. That's something I found it very difficult to cope with, and I would classify what he went through as the male menopause. He started getting very vain and brushing his hair forwards and there was this other woman . . . so he's not cuddly for me, I can't think of him like that although I'm quite cuddly with other people, which is partly the reason I say it's not a father–daughter relationship anymore, it's more of a friendship.'

Ian is aware of Louise's physical reticence and is trying to analyse the current state of their relationship:

'There are no tensions between us now, only when it comes to the physical side of the relationship. She will kiss me on the cheek because she thinks that's the thing to do but the initiative doesn't come from her. I can't honestly tell if she likes me. I like her as a person, more than I feel I love her like a daughter but it's something I'm not sure if she reciprocates, we're not on as good terms as that yet, it's more complicated. . . . I've always loved her, I see no reason for me to change my feelings for her, whereas she has. I'm sure a daughter finds it difficult to forgive a father for doing what I've done, maybe she'll never forgive me. I think underneath it all she will always feel betrayed by what she sees as my action towards her mother. . . . But even in the last few weeks we've become somewhat closer because she's got her first flat and wants me to help to put up some shelves. There's more of an involvement now but I don't think I could just go round there and barge in, but now she's away from the family home it's easier to start to relate to her again. The relationship is being rebuilt, but it's not quite there yet.'

Louise too would like their relationship to become more taken for granted:

'I'd like our relationship to be more easy-going, that he feels relaxed enough to just turn up at my place and I can put the kettle on and we can have a cup of coffee. I don't feel that relaxed about going to his place maybe because he might have someone there, a woman, I don't know, he just doesn't involve me. I'd like a more relaxed footing but I don't really want it getting any heavier.'

Reflecting on her relationship with her father, Louise adds her voice to a now familiar issue: she feels that her father does not talk about feelings in the same way as herself:

'I don't think he'd like me talking about it in this way, he doesn't tend to talk about it, and like a lot of men he doesn't express his emotions very much, that's often part of the problem. I think that's part of why marriages break up because the men don't express their emotions, the release doesn't get out. We don't talk deeply or emotionally about anything.'

Ian confirms this in describing the different kind of relationship that he has with his son James:

'I've got a better relationship with my son, there's more under-standing I think, and I sort of don't regard him as my son, more as a very young brother, and I think he sometimes sees me as an older brother. He tells me about his girlfriends and I suppose I've done the same. I wouldn't do that as far as my daughter's concerned, I don't feel there's the same closeness, the same camaraderie, it's comparing notes I suppose. I don't talk about feelings, though I suppose I have talked to James about my feelings particularly in regard to the last couple of years, whereas I wouldn't feel I could do that with my daughter. . . . I don't feel I could talk to her about emotional things, I don't feel comfortable enough.'

Relationships characterised by male camaraderie are not usually very expressive of emotions and feelings, although these may be obliquely referred to. In defending themselves from the possibility of painful feelings, men find easier recourse in cutting themselves off from their emotions, as Ian did after his departure from the family:

'I've got this facility to be able to blank out for a while, to cut out, although it's there in the background and I still feel the loss and the gap.'

Although these two father–daughter relationships have both illustrated some negative effects of separation, as I emphasised earlier this does not have to be the case. There are many other family separations in which good relationships have been main-tained through fathers (and their daughters if they are old enough) putting time and effort into them.

LONE FATHER AND DAUGHTER RELATIONSHIPS

'I think for single parents it's a much tougher game because you haven't got the resources of another adult to fall back on from time to time, and very strong aggression is very difficult to deal with. She's said some very violent things.'

Tom

*'I think when two parents are together you don't get quite as close
to either of them, because they're a couple, as you do when they're
a single unit. They have that bond together and that will stay when
you've left the nest.'*

Louise

In Britain, the United States and many other developed countries
today, the family has become an unstable unit which frequently
fragments into various forms, usually lone parents and families
containing step-parents. The number of lone-parent families in the
UK has doubled over the last two decades and the proportion of
those that are lone fathers has increased to more than one in ten.
Lone fathering tends to be more transient than lone mothering:
lone fathers generally marry sooner; they are generally caring for
older children; and they are less likely to be full-time at home. It
can be incredibly hard to be a lone parent, both economically and
psychologically. The dynamics are obviously different in one-
parent and in two-parent families: the balance of power has
changed. Lone parents, especially those with younger children,
have no-one to share responsibility with or fall back on for
support. If parents are united, they present a joint front and there
is some measure of distance between parents and children on
opposite sides of the family equation. In families where parents
have separated, and mothers or fathers are living alone with their
children for all or part of the time, different kinds of relationships
can develop. These may be positive and negative. For instance, it
may be difficult for a lone parent to maintain control over a strong-
willed teenager; on the other hand, it is possible that closer
relationships are built up between child and parent. Having only
one parent to negotiate with may provide the opportunity for
greater closeness, equality and solidarity. Problems and issues
which might normally be confined to the realm of parents may be
shared more openly between parent and child.

Less hierarchical relationships can develop between lone parents
and their children. This can involve simple but basic decisions such
as how to organise living space. Peter and his fourteen-year-old
daughter Melanie live together every alternate week in Peter's flat.
When he moved in, they shared the process of creating their own
domestic space, more like a married couple. Peter recalls:

'I said "This is the flat we're going to live in, how do you want to
arrange it?" Things like that, taking decisions for ourselves, were

probably very important. Most of the things that go on in my house I give her some sort of choice over.'

There are a variety of ways that childcare can be divided between separated parents. This inevitably means that there will be periods of discontinuity when parent and children don't see each other. Depending on the nature of the arrangement, this can have the advantage of providing opportunities for numerous fresh starts and the pleasure of seeing someone again. It also means that if a good feeling has built up, this has to be put on hold and then renewed. Peter and Melanie see each other every other week. He comments:

'When Melanie arrives on Sunday afternoon I suddenly feel invaded although I look forward to her coming, so we scrap around that for a day or so. By the end of the week it gets a bit tense because I've got to organise, or she's got to organise herself to move out again. But as a system it works very well. Last week when she was round was absolutely brilliant, we had a great week. Two or three people came for dinner, we went out for a night somewhere else, spent a lot of time talking, a really exciting week, and now it's gone. I've got to start again next Sunday. I think I miss that continuing to build up. Though when it's a bad week I'm kind of glad to get rid of her and she's probably glad to see the back of me, and we can start afresh the next Sunday, so it's definitely swings and roundabouts.'

The balance and stability of a lone-parent family is more likely to be interrupted by the possibility of the parent meeting a new partner. This can be the cause of jealousy and conflict between parent and children. Peter had recently started a new relationship (with Lyn) and felt nervous about the effect this might have on his daughter:

'Melanie was quite sensitive about it. . . . I kept her informed about what was going on between me and Lyn. I think that's been really important for both of us. Lyn's accepted and that's made me very happy. I don't think she felt jealous about me getting involved with anyone else. I haven't really thought about jealousy. No, I think she gives me enough space. I don't think it's adversely affected our relationship at all. It's just lucky she's very mature for her years.'

On this subject Melanie commented:

'It was okay, weird at first. I don't really mind if he has a girlfriend. He's very soppy though and I tease him. I don't feel jealous. Sometimes we go out together, we get on quite well. . . . But I'd prefer it just the two of us living together, I'd feel that somebody was intruding if someone else came to live with us. But I don't think he will, and it's a bit small this flat. I don't worry about it. He might do it after I've left home. I think he knows I like it with just him and me.'

The reverse situation has not yet had to be confronted. Melanie herself has not yet had a boyfriend, and Peter anticipates it with some reservations:

'I suppose at some stage she'll bring boys back. And she'd feel very odd about bringing them back to my flat and exposing her boyfriend to me, and what that would do to me. I think I'd feel, oh, that's it, I'm out the window now. And I'm not sure she's going to choose anybody nice, but that's just prejudice. I suppose in some ways – to keep the relationship analogy – I suppose I'm somehow her boyfriend. This whole part of us is boyfriend and girlfriend. Not lovers obviously but how we argue and sort things out. I think she'd be very wary for both our sakes about bringing another man into that situation . . . but I don't think I feel threatened by it. I'm very intrigued about what she's going to do. I'm far more worried about her than about my reaction to it all.'

Tom is also a lone father. He lives with his fourteen-year-old step-daughter Paula and his daughter Kim. Their mother lives nearby with her husband and new baby but the girls prefer to spend most of their time with their father, who works as a teacher. Unlike Melanie, Paula and Kim have not had to contend with their father becoming involved in another relationship. They claim that they would like Tom to get married, and that they have occasionally tried to matchmake him but without success. This conflicts with Tom's view, that they have appeared to obstruct any plans he makes to go out:

'I don't think it's an accident that I've never got married since. I very rarely go out but every time I do, there's some sort of scene takes place at home. I think the conflict comes more from Paula than from Kim, and of course it's a real difficulty for a single parent and it gets more difficult the older children get. I haven't had a relationship for ten years. I think it's very difficult to establish a relationship when there are kids around.'

Children can also provide the perfect excuse for a lone parent who is not having nor seeking a relationship.

Paula and Kim were young when Tom and their mother split up. Paula's mother is from Trinidad, and she left Paula there as a baby while she was in England, where she met Tom. Through Tom's instigation Paula came to England and they all lived together for a while, and Paula's half-sister Kim was born. Then following a separation, during which time Tom cared for the children, their mother took the children back to Trinidad until Paula was about six. After a persistent pursuit from Tom, and their return from the Caribbean, Tom gained reponsibility for both children, a position he has enjoyed for the last eight years. Paula and Kim were not given a choice then of who to live with, but if they had one now, on balance it would be their father. Paula says she gets on well with her mother, but she is quite clear who she prefers living with:

'I suppose dads are more fun than mums. I suppose when sometimes boys stay with their mum, they get more attached to their mum because they haven't seen their dad so much. But I think girls, if they are with their dad they have more opportunity of getting somewhere in life because their dads respect them, and they can get on even though they are girls. Sex shouldn't make a difference, girl or boy. A lot of my friends prefer their dads. Most of their mums think they should be a nurse or something but they want to be mechanics and stuff like that, it's all changed round! A lot of people whose parents have divorced live with their dads, we've got three girls with their dads and they think it's brilliant, yes, I think living with your dad is best.'

Her sister Kim also prefers being with her father:

'He's just a really nice person to live with, nice as a dad . . . he's cuddly, that's what I like about him. Lots of other people perhaps want cuddles from their dads but they won't and they get annoyed, but my dad cuddles. He's just different from anybody else, that's what I like about him, he's not a boring personality like anybody else. . . . Things I do with my mum, I usually go out or stay at home and watch TV and stuff. With my dad we do more adventurous things like sometimes we write stories together and

Like lone parenting, step-parenting has increased significantly in countries such as the United States, Britain and many European countries, as families divide and reassemble with different fathers and mothers. It has many obvious pitfalls, as step-mothers and step-fathers take on the roles of their 'natural' predecessors.[3] Tom and Paula describe some of their experiences. Tom is unusual in being both a lone father and a step-father, and their non-biological relationship is accentuated by him being white and Paula being black. Step-parenting, like lone parenting, can question things we take for granted. For instance, whether there is anything essential to the relationship between a child and their biological ('real') father that cannot be substituted for? In this context, can a step-father replace a natural father? Clearly this can happen when children are adopted at a young age, but step-parents usually enter children's lives when relationships with natural parents have already been established. There are however some children who hardly know their natural father and have grown up with a step-father for so long that he is equivalent to their 'real' father in every way except inherited genes. Others have to accommodate a step-parent later in their lives and the intensity and characteristics of the relationship they have together will depend on many individual aspects of themselves and their situation. Step-parents find themselves negotiating many kinds of family situations, depending on the age of the children involved and the family's history, as well as basic factors such as whether they and the children like each other. The role of a step-father or step-mother is not an easy one, and the fifty per cent divorce rate amongst step-families in Britain reflects this.

In Tom's family, he is Kim's natural father, while Paula's natural father is in Trinidad. Although Paula hardly knew her father, it is still one of her ambitions to go back there one day and see what he is like. There is a romantic image attached to finding 'real' parents who have disappeared some time early in life. Paula's position is quite a complex one, as Tom describes:

'Now that her mum has remarried and got a child of her own she rather uses Paula as a sort of childminder for the child, whereas what Paula really wants is to be the special one of her mum, and regardless of how special she's always been to me, it's not what she wants, now that she's aware of who she is and the relationships between everybody. She wants the security of knowing there's one person who she belongs to. It's a curious position for her to be in. Her father she knows of, but doesn't know; her mother she doesn't live with. She lives with me and I'm not a blood relative of hers. But I've made choices and decisions all the way along to try and confirm for her that she's special for me.'

If you are a step-parent, your authority is undermined by not being a child's 'real' parent, however long or strong your relationship has been with the children. This is used by children as verbal ammunition to resist the control of their step-parents, or used between a child and her or his step-sister or step-brother. This had been Tom's experience, and it can be hurtful:

'Paula uses the fact that I'm not her real father in her anger, it comes out on every occasion when a certain pressure point has been passed. I actually find it very hard to take. Every time it happens I feel angry about it. When I attempt to compare what I've offered for both of them I think the offer is as equal as it could be and I feel sad that Paula can't accept it the way that it is, otherwise she wouldn't come back to that, she'd drop that argument, she'd use something else. I think until she does she can have this constant excuse for everything being not quite right in her life. Whenever anything goes wrong she can fall back and say "I had a wicked step-father." I've reached the point on a number of occasions of saying, "Okay, if that's what you want, take the option you're advocating." It would touch me if it did actually happen and she left home, but the actual pain she wreaks at times is so great I think, "Let me be free of this." And the fact that her mother doesn't get any of this is also extremely painful to me, because I have the impression that most of this is actually directed at her mother for not looking after her because that option was always there. . . . Also there was a lot of jealousy with Paula and Kim, and Kim used to play the thing up from time to time, not in tangible ways, but she used to refer to "my dad" – the implication being that I wasn't Paula's dad.'

In some ways, Tom finds it difficult having his daughters' mother living nearby. She represents a court of appeal on his decisions about Paula, which can also undermine his authority. Tom believes it would have helped if Paula had made her own choice of who she wanted to live with when she was younger:

'On reflection I would have preferred Paula to spend time with her mother until such time as she would have decided of her own volition and choice to come here. I think that would have changed the chemistry of the relationship in a way that would have made life much easier for both of us. If her mum hadn't been there she would have had to face up to the fact that I was being as fair as I could to both of them. I would be the end of the line.'

Both step-fathers and daughters may have an awareness of not being blood-related and Tom had found that this implicitly created a measure of physical distance between them, which is not the case with his 'real' daughter Kim:

'Kim is incredibly cuddly, so it's impossible not to be cuddly with Kim around. But I've never worried about that, I've always felt secure about it. I've obviously been aware of some sort of need for distancing with Paula – she's not my own child. And like the question of getting into bed together for instance, I've felt slightly different rules ought to apply to Paula. But Paula's never allowed herself to be my little girl, well that's not quite true, but certainly she's very clearly detached from that role. It's a sadness to me that the relationship isn't the same, but at some stage Paula has deliberately distanced herself. I sometimes worry about the sort of relationships she will have with boys. I think it will be a reflection of the kind of relationship she has manufactured with me.'

It also reflects the way in which the incest taboo operates between 'natural' fathers and daughters, but does not have the same power in a step-father situation, leaving Tom extra aware of the physical and sexual parameters of their relationship.

As a daughter in this situation, Paula is more critical of Tom than she is of her mother because he is the one with whom she comes into everyday contact. She is very aware of him not being her real father, but she ultimately appreciates everything he is trying to do for her. She describes their relationship:

'I get on more with my mum than my dad, because we have arguments about little things. It starts off with homework then it ends up with everything altogether, and I say "Why are you saying this, you're not my real father", things like that. It gets out of hand a bit . . . because I'm not his daughter really, I don't get special treatment, but I do have a special sense in a way that I do have things differently. . . . If he were my real father it would be different. I don't see him like a proper father, I just see him like a boss at home. Maybe he wouldn't be so over-protective, because I can't leave and he's got custody over me. . . . But I don't mind my dad telling me what time I have to come in, because I know it's because he wants to know I'm safe and everything. And I think my real dad would say, "Who cares, do what you like", and I'd probably end up on drugs or smoking hemp or something! I suppose if there were no rows I get on better with my dad really.'

Paula has contradictory feelings: she holds the idea that a 'proper' father might do things differently, yet she is well aware that her father in Trinidad cares for her much less than Tom does. There is always the hope that the father we do not know will be the ideal father, while we criticise the human failings of the father we know.

Whatever the nature of Paula's arguments with Tom, and her relationship with her mother, Tom is a very significant person in her life. A different situation is illustrated by Alice, who has had three different father-figures in her life but feels she has not really got a father at all. She is a sixteen-year-old dance and drama student and has grown up in the north west of England in a working-class family, currently consisting of her mother and eldest brother. Alice's real father, who was half-Italian, left when she was very small; then from the age of four until quite recently she had a step-father, but she never felt very close to him and the relationship he had with Alice's mother has since ended. Now her mother has met a new boyfriend with whom she is having a serious relationship. Alice describes how she feels:

'I don't feel like I've got a father. I've got more fathers than anybody else really, but if I had to say who was my father I couldn't answer. My mum's boyfriend is becoming my father, but he will never be my father; and with my step-father, I felt a bit difficult through the divorce. I guess I loved him as a father then, but now I don't as much as I did because of everything my mum's been through. Now he's gone to Tenerife and he's stopped writing. And my real father I just can't have a real conversation with, so I don't class him as a father.'

Alice has a close relationship with her second brother, but the one consistent person in her life is her mother, who she loves and respects as a parent. She may have had step-fathers, but for Alice, her family is essentially headed by her mother, as she describes:

'My mum's like the boss, and if my real father says to me. "You can't do that", I say "You've got no authority over me, because you might be my father but you've never known me." But if my mum says something I jump and do it. I guess I took it from my step-father when he said something serious, but really it's always my mum. My mum's more important to me than anybody apart from my brother, and if anybody's going to hurt her, I'm not going to take their side.'

Attention gets mainly focused on problems in relationships between step-parents and children when children are young and there may be tussles about things like discipline and authority. These disappear or become less significant when children have grown up and made separate lives of their own. There may still, however, be issues to address and Sally, now thirty-one, has been giving a lot of recent thought to the question of which of the two father-figures in her life she felt was really her father. She has had a step-father from the age of eight, and he has been the loving father she has known for most of her life. When she was about seven, Sally and her parents and younger sister moved to Barbados where her father had taken a planning job. It was there that he started to drink and the marriage broke up soon after. Both parents subsequently remarried in Barbados and after some time Sally and her mother, step-father and sister returned to England where her mother had two more children. Sally and her sister visited their father occasionally in Barbados, until he eventually returned to England having separated from his second wife. Still a heavy drinker, he was in and out of hospital and hostels until he was allocated a flat. Sally does not enjoy spending time with him, nor does she respect him, but she feels responsible for him in some way because he is her 'real' father and she is the only person who does anything for him. She comments: 'Whatever he does, however he behaves, he is still my biological father and I feel I should not lose touch with him.'

Recently, the nature and definition of fatherhood has became an issue for both herself and her sister, as Sally explains:

'My father has been upset because my sister is getting married in June but has told my father that she wants our step-father to give her away. Having been brought up from the age of six by our step-father she feels he is more of a father than her natural father. I had an equal number of years with each and can remember life with my father, unlike my sister. It does raise the question with us though about what is a father? Is it the person who fathered you or is it the person who brought you up and acted as your father? I sometimes wonder why I feel a sense of guilt and responsibility towards my real father, who I don't dislike but whom I find very uninteresting and whom it is a sense of duty to visit rather than a pleasure. I do not feel proud of my father and am quite envious of friends who have smart, professional, good-looking fathers who take an interest in their daughters. My mother would say I have such a father – my step-father – and I think she finds it upsetting that I do not see him more as a father.'

In Sally's situation, her step-father and father are not in competition: they occupy very different positions in her life. She regrets that her father is not someone she can really love or respect:

'I would really love my father to be the kind of person I wanted to spend more time with. The kind of person I could invite to stay for weekends and to go to films with. He is not a person I like to spend more than a couple of hours with. He rarely asks me about myself or friends and only talks about things such as his latest clothes bargains from Oxfam – it is very sad.'

Nevertheless, the knowledge that he is her father means that Sally cannot ignore him. We usually have little choice over the members of our family. Our biological parents, brothers and sisters are linked to us by definition, whether or not we like them. But if you have experienced more than one person in your life who has acted as a mother or father to you, why should your 'real' parent have precedence? Such parents are not always the best people to bring up their children (a view which is reinforced by the number of neglected and abused children in society), and many of us would benefit from having more than one close father- or mother-figure in whom we could trust and confide.

The characteristics of a good father–daughter relationship that women and men described at the beginning of the chapter, such as concern with closeness, communication, affection, mutual respect and tolerance, are not the sole prerogative of daughter and father relationships. They can apply similarly to many other sorts of relationships. But they are significant in reflecting the high levels of emotional involvement that many daughters have with their fathers and their often unsatisfied desires to receive something similar in return. The girls and women participating in the last three sections of this chapter have various kinds of relationship with men who have taken some sort of father role in their lives. They indicate that it is the nature and quality of the relationship that counts, rather than the biological tie; or the quantity of time spent together; or whether or not a child is cared for by its mother. Thus, the father and daughter situations illustrated here show that a positive father–daughter relationship does not necessarily depend on having an 'ideal' family structure (the 'nuclear family'); that lone fathers may become both father and mother to their daughters; and that it is possible for step-fathers to take the same role as 'real' fathers. All of this suggests that both fathering and mothering in our society are largely socially constructed.

Chapter 7

Ageing: the roles reverse

'I remember when my dad was seventy and I was thirty-five, really seeing that he was an old man, but I have this memory of a person who wasn't like that at all.'

Rosemary

'The only frailness I feel is the fact I can't lift what I used to, I can't work as fast as I used to. But I don't see Rosemary looking after me, that would never do! I'd definitely kick over the traces there. I don't mind bossing her around, but I'm not going to have her bossing me around. No, I'd hate to be dependent on her.'

Stanley

'During the last ten years of his life, the caring roles were reversed, as Father was assailed first with Mother's failing health; then her death, and finally the frailty of his own old age, culminating in senility. The wheel had come full circle: my feelings for him were by this time much more akin to the nurturing ones I felt towards my own children and indeed he had become a sweet and gentle old man.'

Jane

Most sons and daughters recognise quite early in life that their parents are only human and make mistakes. They have feelings and emotions like anyone else, and they are not right in everything they do and say. Although parents are supposed to take care of their children, this relationship may be quite fluid, and care and protection may move in either direction at different times in our lives. For illustration, Richard and Sophie's relationship has been described for many other reasons, and at the age of fifty-four and nineteen respectively, Richard feels that their relationship has already passed through several such stages:

'I suppose you could argue that our relationship has gone through a series of changes. To begin with I was the father and she was the daughter. Then we were like brother and sister really. And I suspect now it's gone right round and she's more like a mother to me, because she tends to keep an eye on me, tries to steer me in the right direction. She is inclined, probably because in some respects I am somewhat of a child, to be a little more mature than I am. So it has gone through this metamorphosis from father and daughter to mother and son almost.'

It is certainly not surprising that many girls and women easily find themselves playing a nurturing role to their fathers, although it may not usually happen as early as with Richard and Sophie. Richard recalls:

'People used to say to me "You spoil that child". And I'd say "I don't. She spoils me." And she did – from when she was four, she would spoil me. If I came in from work and I was really down, she would come over to me – and we're talking of a girl of about eight or nine – and say "Come on, you look as though you're down, you need a cuddle." Just as if I was the child.'

Sophie affirmed her desire to look after her father:

'I'm quite protective over him. He hasn't been well for the last year or so, which makes it very difficult for him. He gets down. I think I'm protective partly against himself, because he's always getting himself down. So someone's got to do it!'

It is painful to watch someone you love, like a parent, growing older and weaker in many ways. Ageing is a one-way process. When you are young it is tempting to think parents will always be strong, they will be able to look after you forever. But as time goes by, both daughters and sons find themselves taking a different view of their fathers, and playing a different role in their lives. For example, one thirty-one-year-old woman wrote about her father: 'He is fragile, vulnerable, emotionally inadequate and feeble. Today I feel like I want to protect him from feeling because I fear it would overwhelm him.' Ageing makes us frailer and more vulnerable. We become aware of mortality, of illness, and death. Some fathers can retain the same strength of personality and

power they have always exerted over their children, but not all
are able to preserve this charismatic quality. The traditional image
of a strong, dominant father is diminished as he is exposed as
another vulnerable human being, often with old-fashioned ideas.
Other fathers mellow gradually with age, glad to be relieved of
some of the responsibility of being a father and family bread-
winner, especially when they retire from work.

Protection becomes the focus now, and is mentioned frequently
as women talk about their ageing fathers, whether it be protecting
them from illness, physical exertion, and family conflict, or simply
because they see fathers getting older and frailer and in need of
general care. This has happened between Margaret and her father
Raymond. Now in her late thirties and with a career in social
research, Margaret has a partner and children of her own.
Although her mother is still fit and well, she realises that she has
already taken on some of her mother's role in respect to Raymond,
who is now sixty-five:

'I'm terribly understanding of my father now. I tiptoe round my
dad. I'm protecting him the way my mother protected him. He
doesn't have to take a lot of things, she does it for him. My mum's
the peacemaker, she tries to stop conflict before it starts. She
protects him from all those things. If my dad gets upset, oh God,
I don't want my father to feel upset, I don't want him to feel hurt.
I just love him a lot. I love my mum a lot as well, but not like
that. I don't protect my mum from being hurt or anything. I feel
she can take it and I don't feel my dad can, he's never had to. I
feel I still want to challenge my mum in some ways but I don't
want to challenge my dad. . . . But perhaps we both protect each
other, perhaps we both feel very delicate about our relationship,
we both want it to be okay.'

Like the daughter above who wanted to protect her father 'from
feeling' because she was afraid it would overwhelm him, Margaret
wants to protect Raymond from being hurt because he is not
used to it, unlike her mother. By recognising or attributing
such emotional vulnerability, it is easy to collude in protecting
and preserving this condition. Although it may be an act of
compassion and love, nevertheless it casts women once again
in the role of supporting men's emotional shortcomings, right
up to the end of their lives. It also relates to the ways
many women constantly make allowances for these kinds of

failings in their fathers, husbands and the other men in their lives.

As the roles of father and daughter may gradually reverse, daughters become aware of being both emotionally and physically stronger, and possibly in a better financial position too. I described in earlier chapters how many women, who like myself grew up in postwar Britain, reaped the advantages of a more egalitarian education system, and progressed through higher education or training to achieve more than either of their parents. Elaine and her two younger sisters, all now in their late thirties and forties, have each gained much more education and income than their father, who spent most of his life employed as a railway fireman. None of them have yet married. Elaine is the eldest at forty-four, and a freelance artist. She reflects on the way her relationship with her parents has changed:

'Our relationship is now different, almost a reverse one. They start almost being your children in a way, as they get more vulnerable. My father's been a creaking gate for years. I parent him more now, and my sisters and I do any lifting or heavy work when he's working at DIY at our homes. . . . The three of us feel quite protective and responsible for our parents. I don't talk to them about problems or worries because in a way I don't want them to worry, so I'm protecting them. . . . I realised years ago that I was more powerful than my father. For years I earned more than he, was more experienced and sophisticated and generally felt a bit embarrassed by him. I think he is an innocent and naïve person by nature, and very kind. I remember at about eleven or twelve feeling responsible for him as he used to pretend to almost fall in the canal where we used to walk and he couldn't swim, whereas I could. I guess we three [sisters] did treat him as a bit of a country bumpkin and shielded him somewhat.'

Other women also commented on these kinds of changes in physical and emotional dependency with ageing. Sonia's sixty-two-year-old father still works hard as a painter and decorator in the Midlands. She is thirty-nine, married with two young daughters and working in neighbourhood development. Although she and her father have had their share of rows and disagreed on political grounds, Sonia is very fond of him: she feels they understand each other and are important to one another. He has always been a source of security for her. She is aware that they have reached another stage in their lives, and writes:

'It is painful to watch my dad grow old and to see him become less competent at the things he has always been good at. Over the years as my social milieu has broadened I have recognised just how unworldly my dad is and just how uninformed and silly a lot of his decisions have been. I now feel very protective towards him and in some ways deeply sorry for this little man who is ageing now quite rapidly. I can't help feeling sad that he is not happier. . . . Even as adults, my dad feels that he has to provide for us in some way. Getting him to receive anything from us, since we have been in a position to give, has been very difficult. During a difficult financial period a few years ago we were in the position to give Dad some money. It was a very emotional time, he just dissolved. Asking for and receiving help has never been a strong point with Dad, and it is something I find difficulty with at times.'

In general, women find it easier than men to seek help, whether it be for health or other personal reasons, and the increasing vulnerability that comes with old age conflicts with the images of masculinity that many men feel they have to conform to. It is no longer so easy (if it ever was) to take the role of a strong, powerful provider, and this can create insecurity and conflict.

The process of ageing can be cause for much personal contemplation on each side of the father–daughter relationship. Some daughters have spoken of how their father's personality seemed to soften or mellow with old age, while others have became more entrenched. Diana, a thirty-six-year-old journalist, has also been giving a lot of thought to these processes of increasing dependency in her relationship with her seventy-three-year-old father, precipitated by his recent illness, She is one of six children who grew up in Scotland. Her father was a gardener and her mother worked as an auxiliary nurse when times were hard, as they often were. She writes:

'As a child I was totally dependent on my parents. Then at seventeen I realised that I had to stand on my own two feet. At eighteen I did so. I made a lot of mistakes in the next few years but survived all of them. . . . Now my parents are dependent on me, and my partner. Not just for the odd cheque – given voluntarily and very willingly – but more for emotional support. They confide things in us (my father especially) which they would not necessarily confide in the others. And they rely on us for moral support. . . . My father and my present partner have a very close relationship, they understand each other, so the three of us have become very close.'

While Diana has moved round the life-cycle into a role of responsibility for her ageing father, Anne is trying to break away from this. She is single and thirty-one-years-old. She has always felt responsible for her father, now aged seventy-four. From when she was small, Anne had been a closer companion to her father than her mother had been. Her parents' relationship was rather estranged and that between Anne and her father caused much hostility between her and her mother. Because of Anne's close involvement with her father, and their interdependency, she is caught in a contradictory position now that he is elderly, because she feels she should be helping him to prepare for dying. This has become more acute since he suffered a stroke:

'I have this thing that I'm frightened to go away because what if he's ill or he dies, how would I feel? But I've been worried about him dying since I can't remember when. I worried about him dying when I was in my teens, I was so sort of caught up with him and responsible for his happiness really. I feel he needs me to help him cope with coming to terms with dying, and I feel frightened by that. . . . I feel I've had lots of rehearsals and it's like me trying to come to terms with that, and not hurting myself so much when it does happen. Preparing myself. So when he did have a stroke it was dreadful, and it felt like emotionally it all fell to me when he was ill. I went up and stayed with my mother. He was in hospital for a fortnight and we went to see him every day. He was terribly needing affection, I think that's quite common in those cases. He wanted me to sit and hold his hand because my mum wouldn't do it, she was embarrassed in public. . . . When I came away and left him in hospital it was like leaving my baby (even though I haven't got any). When I eventually came home when he was better he sat in bed and wept. It's making me cry again remembering. How the roles reverse!'

Conflicting with these feelings are Anne's present desire to break free and pursue things for herself, and getting a job in a different field (leaving probation work to become an advocate) has been part of this process and has given her more confidence:

'I'm now thinking, right, I'm entitled to my own life. I've never really felt that. I felt that my life belonged to him really . . . that it fell to me and not to any of the others. So for me to move jobs, it's been quite a big thing. I've walked away from my profession, gone off and done something related but very different. It's not insignificant that this came at a time when my dad's been ill and everything's changing in the family dynamics. I've suddenly realised that I've got a lot of energy, and I'm going to do what I want to do. Part of the resolution process will be acclimatising [my parents] to that. My fear is, I don't want my dad to feel betrayed. I don't want him to feel that I'd be leaving him when he's frightened of dying. I very much feel that he wants to travel that path with me in some way. He wants me to protect him again.'

Elderly men may experience both physical and sometimes intellectual vulnerability, especially if changes in present-day ideas and technology make parts of their past knowledge redundant. For some fathers this may feel threatening but for others, relinquishing the need to know everything may make them more relaxed and open, creating the potential for a more equal parent–child relationship. Freed from the pressures of the workplace or a family to provide for, fathers may become more accessible and communicative within the family. Illness may also have this effect. For Kate, now twenty-eight, the early relationship with her father had never been close or communicative and she had felt very rejected from adolescence when her interest in boys seemed to trigger his angry withdrawal from her life, but traumatic illness in his latter years had suddenly changed the way he interacted with her:

'My relationship with dad has changed – he is much more mellow, still very dominant and moody with mum, but generally very much more relaxed and easy to be with. I can talk to dad and we can feel quite close although he has often silently disapproved of things I've done. I honestly feel he has respect for who I am and what I am capable of. The change was quite gradual until last year when he was minutes from death. He had a successful life-saving by-pass operation and has been able to show more closeness and warmth since then.'

It is good that such changes can occur but it seems sad if there are many similar men who have to wait until they face their own mortality before they are better able to recognise and express such basic feelings and emotions.

Death, like sex, may be a taboo subject of conversation in some families. Getting older, becoming ill or dying are issues that people don't like to talk about very much. Parents and children often avoid speaking of death almost superstitiously, thinking that if you don't talk about it maybe it won't happen, or simply not wanting to be the one to suggest anything so morbid. But this means that children don't really know how their parents feel about these issues and how they would like things to be when they do arise. Barbara is a teacher in her late twenties, with a husband and baby daughter, and although she feels very caring for both her parents, she feels this gap in understanding with John, her father, who is now seventy:

'It's very depressing, parents getting older. I don't know what it's like to be old. There's a barrier as well, as I don't know how he feels about it. I think it's very sad, in the fairly near future he'll get very old and die. It's hard to imagine what life will be like without him. He's not the sort of person to be very good at being very ill and very old. But it's strange not knowing how he feels about it and not being able to ask him. We're both trying to protect one another. If you showed me everything he said, we might get some communication!

'I think I'm at the stage now of the awareness of parents' problems, that there's a changeover state. I think some people are much closer in a sense to their parents. My parents never argued in front of us and I grew up with this idea that they were happy and contented and didn't have worries of their own. Now I think I'm at the stage where I realise that they have their own problems, and although they don't need looking after at the moment as they're still independent, I suppose it does change.'

Barbara has three older sisters, all married with children, and believes they would all be wanting to look after their father. Although John himself also realises this, he wants to keep his independence as long as possible and he is not really sure that he would really enjoy fitting in with their ways of running their homes and children. His response to the possibility was:

'The problem of old age is terrible. I don't want to be looked after by my daughters. . . . I don't really want to live with any of them, it would upset their lives and I can't stand the carry on.'

It is a common assumption that children should look after their parents in old age; it is after all some recompense for all the work their parents have put into bringing them up. But neither side is necessarily in favour of this: parents are often afraid of losing their independence and being a burden to their children; and their children may find it difficult to care for them either financially, practically or psychologically. Sometimes an elderly parent coming to live with his or her daughter or son can drive either or both generations to distraction. The way the social structure and ideology combines to make women the major carers in society means that the burden of looking after old people generally falls to them. It is women who work in old people's homes, and it is daughters who predominately find themselves caring for their elderly parents. The traditional role of the unmarried daughter in caring for elderly parents and other elderly relatives has a firm place in history and is still common today. Current government policy is to cut financial support to old people's homes and other caring facilities, and replace it by care in the community. This is immediately translated into care in the family, and it is women on whose shoulders this care falls. Even if fathers or mothers go to live with their sons, it is invariably the daughter-in-law who organises their day-to-day care as the division of domestic labour in the home still falls predominantly on women.

While Barbara and her three sisters would have no objections to looking after their parents, other daughters are less enthusiastic. Neither Margaret nor her father Raymond (quoted earlier) are keen that he should ever end up living with her and her family. She feels, like many other daughters in this position today, that she wants to be free to lead her own life:

'I want to pursue what I want to do, and that's terribly selfish in some ways, but that's what I want. I would resent it, I would hate it, to have to look after my parents. . . . But would I be able to put my mum and dad into a home? I'd feel terrible. I just hope they kick their bucket before they need looking after. I would hope that too, for my own kids, I would hate them to look after me.'

Raymond is equally dubious about the prospect, and worries about becoming a burden to either of his two daughters:

'I'm sure that's when our relationship would come to a sticky end! I would hope they would [look after me], knowing the two as I do, I'm quite sure that they would want to. I wouldn't like to think that they were not going to look after me, but who can tell? At the moment though, I'm not going to be a burden to my children. I would hope that I never have to rely on them. Not that I wouldn't want what they have to offer me, it's simply that they've got their lives to get on with and they would be encumbered by somebody who is doddery and a nuisance.'

In western society we do not treat older people with the same respect and veneration found in many other societies. We tend to devalue them rather than learning from them, placing more emphasis on the energy and working power of young people. It is part of the ideology of a consumer and disposable society, which puts false positive values on the young and the new and tends to automatically dismiss anything old. In this respect, John at seventy compares himself with the husbands of his four daughters, who are of course a lot younger, and this accentuates any sense of inadequacy that the ageing process brings:

'I don't mind getting older with daughters, but with the husbands I hate it because it's different – like driving faster, being out of date. I don't like it. It's nice to feel you've lived a long time, had a lot of experience in some ways you can be treated as a guru.'

The problem of caring for elderly people in our society is an increasing one, as people live longer and the proportion of old people in the population steadily rises. Should it be a duty for children to look after their ageing parents? It is something that certainly provokes guilt, especially in women who are brought up to feel they have to care for the people who need them such as their children or their parents. But even daughters or sons who have a good relationship with their parents are not necessarily the best people to look after them in old age. If the father–daughter relationship has been a very mixed one, as in the case of Yvonne, it can generate equally mixed feelings when a father is old and helpless. Yvonne is an only child. Her father was great fun to be with when she was a child and she adored him, but she felt she could never please him (apart from providing him with grand-children), and he would never praise her to her face. He could also be very cruel and verbally hurtful to her and her mother and Yvonne is aware of the irony of this in his present condition:

'Now my father has Alzheimer's disease. The first thing he lost was his speech. My mother asked me once "Do you ever think about how often he was cruel with his tongue?" I had, but I don't believe in divine retribution. The disease has taken more of a hold now. My mother is exhausted looking after him as she has been throughout their marriage. I sometimes wonder if she enjoys the power she has now though. For the first time she can do as she likes within the limits of being a carer.

'I looked after him recently while she had a break. He was like a child. He is quite happy for me to wash him, etc. He has no embarrassment. I find my feelings are very confused now. He needs me to help him. I look at his face and find it so hard to believe nothing is happening behind his expression. I keep thinking how appalled he would have been at the thought of my doing what I am now doing with him. Sometimes I think he has been a problem to me all my life and has found a way to continue to be one until the day he dies! I wonder why I should look after him? What is duty? Has he fulfilled his duty to me? Then I think back to riding on the crossbar of his bike to the allotment. I was four years old but I remember it vividly. We'd stop at a pub with a garden for lemonade on the way home. He'd take each of my hands in his to wash them – no-one made as many soapy bubbles as he did, it felt so good. Now when he sees me, he holds my hands and looks at me. The last words he was able to say were I love you. Love is all he has left now. I shall look after him, of course. Not out of duty, I don't know why. Because he's my father?'

As well as being principally responsible for caring for other people in society, women are usually far better able to look after themselves than the majority of men. Women also live longer than men, so it is just as well they are better able to survive. Elaine (quoted earlier) agrees, with respect to her own elderly parents: 'If my father was left on his own he would find it more difficult than if my mother was. She'd be able to cope more both emotionally and practically.' It means too, that there are a lot more elderly mothers alive than fathers so there is more likelihood that their children will find themselves caring (if they do at all) for their elderly mother or mother-in-law than for their father or father-in-law.

As young men and women grow up and become more physically and intellectually mature, many find that they overtake their parents by growing larger, stronger or more knowledgeable and powerful in the world outside the family. The increasing confidence that this brings makes it easier to challenge parental authority and other aspects of the parent–child relationship. But challenging such established and complex relationships is not a simple task. Even though both father and daughter/son now theoretically have an equal adult status, parental roles and ingrained ways of interacting stand firm, and the relationship retains many of its childhood characteristics. For instance, Fiona (aged thirty-two) has described in Chapters 2 and 6 how she has always felt unsatisfied with the relationship she has had with her father David, especially the lack of closeness between them. He has remained a strong presence in her life even though he left her mother when Fiona and her sisters were very small, and has always maintained a careful distance between himself and his children. Fiona has many times planned to challenge him and tell him what she really feels but, even though she now has a partner and children of her own, she has still been unable to do so. Now David is in his sixties and in her eyes potentially less strong and powerful than he used to be, she feels she has left it too late and is afraid of her own power to hurt him:

'After I'd had some psychotherapy, one of the things I wanted to do was to see him on his own, so I arranged to go for a meal with him, and was going to say all these things, and it was just pathetic. I was just listening to him, laughing, thinking, "You're really nice" and I never got round to saying anything. I think I was taken in by his charm really, plus now that he's getting older, he's sixty-eight or something, and he's been really ill although he's better now. So I started thinking, "Christ, he's going to die and I haven't sorted it all out with him". He's a bit fumbly now whereas he used to be powerful and attractive. He's still attractive, but he's vulnerable and in a way I can't bear that either. . . . I think my fancy has been I'm going to tell him, I'm going to make him cry, tell him where he's gone wrong and what a bastard he'd been and he can't get away with being like this to women. He's got all these daughters, all these wives, and I'll make him vulnerable and pathetic. But now that he's getting vulnerable himself I can't bear it, I would be the horrible one. So it was going to be like "You're getting your come-uppance", but when it actually came to it, I couldn't do it, and I don't think I ever will really. Unless I just say it, and then I'll feel so guilty that it's not worth the guilt. And then he'll die, and I'll be seeing a therapist for the next fifty years! I'd rather be the martyr.'

If a father has exerted a dominant, even tyrannical role in his daughter's (or son's) life, this may continue until he dies, and may never be challenged. In Stella's case, her eighty-two-year-old father still retains a very strong presence and can very easily upset her. He spent his life in the army and the family moved wherever his work took him. Stella is now forty-nine and has been married three times, a situation to which she believes her father–daughter relationship has contributed. She deeply resents the unfair treatment she feels she has had from him throughout her life, his lack of recognition of herself and her achievements, especially in comparison to her sister. Nevertheless, she has always seen him as a good father and this leaves her with very contradictory feelings. She writes:

'I love him dearly too. I recognise we are very alike, both irascible and judgemental; and that he was a very loving "papa" to my youngest daughter when her father dropped out of her life. He is also capable of extreme generosity and has never, ultimately, let me down in the important things. But sometimes I am impatient that he is still alive, still in control – that I can't put him in the past, and step out from his shadow.'

When we are faced with the death of our father, the feelings we have will obviously be very dependent on the nature of the relationship. As with anyone close to us who dies, unless there is some preparation beforehand there is usually a lot left unsaid. In the case of fathers and daughters, there may be much unknown as well as unsaid. I sometimes wish I had talked to my own father about our relationship before he died, but I suspect that even with the perfect opportunity, we might both have still avoided this. I felt that in some ways he never really knew me because he created his own ideal image of me and we skirted around issues that we radically disagreed about. I colluded in this deception, but there was enough I did to please him that made everything all right and he was very proud of me. It seems sad but I think he knew that I loved him and that I always appreciated the things he did for me.

If there is time to prepare for losing someone, this can be very valuable. Diana (quoted earlier in the chapter) wrote to me when she was very worried about her seventy-three-year-old father, who was very ill. She has always been close to him, and feels that she is very like him in many ways. For her, writing about him at this time was a way of reflecting on and consolidating their relationship:

'Two years ago my father had his first heart attack. He is now seriously ill, and last week I took what may or may not be my final leave of him. We were both in tears as he told me his love for me was indestructible. So is mine for him. It's not easy facing the death of a parent, especially a parent one loves. It is very much a time of reflection. Hence all these pages. It makes you realise how much you love someone, how much you gain from them. When he dies, who will tell me how to treat a clematis, or tell me stories about life in a Scottish tenement? But at least my partner and I have assembled something like six hours of tape of him talking about his life, and endlessly philosophising. So I will have something. I won't just have him. Then it'll be down to me.'

The power of the father can diminish with age, but the father– daughter relationship does not necessarily become any simpler. Fathers become potentially vulnerable in old age: daughters become protective, extending the caring role they have already taken with their children. Their roles have moved into reverse. Illness becomes life-threatening, the prospect of death is closer and frightening and men's emotions may be drawn to the surface. Both they and their daughters may be stimulated to reflect on and even talk about the nature of their past and present relationship. Some fathers become more open, others dominate their daughter until the end. Death does not necessarily provide release for the one left behind. Alongside a collection of personal memories, daughters may be also left with a legacy of unresolved issues and unspoken words.

Chapter 8

Concluding thoughts

'It's lovely to have a child to carry your name on, but not really to be involved in it. I felt that you shouldn't be too close. My three wives and all the women I've been involved with tell me you cannot do things on reason and that I undervalue emotion, and feelings that cannot be put into words.'

David

'Our daughters have given [my husband] enormous pleasure and family life is very important to him. Like me he feels that it is probably easier and more pleasurable to rear two strong young women than softer sensitive young men.'

Sonia

The sheer volume of correspondence that I received from daughters wishing to help me in my research, as well as its content, leaves no doubt about the strength and intensity of the effects that fathers can have on their daughters. In their turn, fathers also testify to the effects that their daughters can have on them, sometimes dramatic, but generally without the equivalent far-reaching consequences.

As small girls in the family, fathers may affect their daughter's development of feminity and the feminine role in various complex ways. Special attachments may be set up between father and daughter, which are very pleasurable but can be problematic if they do not eventually allow girls the space to develop their own separate identities. Fathers can be particularly important in giving praise and recognition of girls' activities and achievements. The role of the father as more powerful, and often more distant means that he, more than their mother, tends to be the parent that a girl wishes to please. Mothers are taken for granted: their love is generally seen as unconditional and therefore worth less, a characteristic reinforced by women's lower status in society. A father's interest, praise and approval can spur his daughter on to greater achievement; and yet his lack of interest may serve to demoralise, or be taken up in some cases as a challenge. The patterns are not set in fixed lines, and there are many individual factors affecting any father–daughter dynamic. From the other side, daughters' achievements can affect their fathers in various ways: some, as we have seen, feel threatened that their female offspring are doing better than they are, while others are delighted that their daughters are taking up the opportunities that they did not have themselves.

The family can be the repository for male violence and women's lives can be physically, sexually and psychologically wrecked by the impact of male physical and sexual abuse. Fortunately, it may still be possible for them to come through this experience and take control of their lives. The subject of sexuality in general is not a comfortable one for fathers and daughters. It is often mutually difficult terrain for conversation or sex education, and when girls begin to mature physically and sexually, their fathers may set some psychological distance between them. Alternatively, it can be young girls themselves who first become aware of the need for their own physical privacy and begin to shut fathers out of the more intimate areas of their lives. Fathers' response to daughters' sexuality reflects men's general attitude to women and part of men's traditional role has been to possess and protect women. A daughter qualifies doubly for this: as female and as offspring. Man is both predator and protector. This is an ambivalent situation for fathers that can result in strict enforcement of sexual morality and over-protection, which may lead to conflict and resistance in their daughters. It may also generate guilt and fears about men and sexuality in those daughters. If, on the other hand, a father gives positive recognition and respect to his daughter as a sexual person, this can help her to create her own sexual identity and confidence.

It is fascinating to try to work out the ways in which our choice of partners, and the relationships we have with them, have been influenced by the characteristics of our fathers and our relationships with them. There may be many and various patterns: women may be attracted to certain characteristics in men and avoid others because these represent their fathers; they may be seeking to reproduce their 'perfect' father, or looking for a lover or husband to replace the father they never had. Men and women change their partners so often in today's society that many different sorts of men may be sampled, rather than repeating a particular formula. Some characteristics, like having a domineering father, can produce opposite tendencies in a daughter: she may be attracted to a domineering man because he is like her father, or she may be repelled for the same reason. She may go from the first to the second. When factors such as violence are involved, a cycle may be set up in which the daughter who has received violence from her father gets involved with a man who is also violent, as Judy did (Chapter 3). But it is possible to break this cycle, as she has done through her own efforts, and eventually therapeutic help. Looking at daughters' choice of partners from the other side, fathers may find it hard to let their daughters go to another man, especially when he is inevitably younger and fitter. This is perhaps more easily accepted under the ritual handing-over in marriage.

Two interesting questions emerge from looking at some of the different situations of fathering. First, whether a man can be a father to girls and boys who are not his own in the same way as a natural father? The answer is basically yes, it is possible, and the number of families with step-parents is steadily increasing. But it is tricky ground and depends on many factors, such as the age of the children, the presence or absence of the real father, and whether the children and step-father like one another. Step-fathers generally have more problems reaching a good relationship with step-daughters than they do with step-sons.

The second question is whether a man can be both father and mother for his children, and specifically his daughters? Lone fathers too are on the increase, and appear as capable at bringing up their sons and daughters as are mothers, despite some attitudes to the contrary. Several teenage girls living with their fathers have told me that they find it easier to talk to their fathers about things like periods and contraception than to their mothers. While the rise in numbers of lone fathers and step-fathers is a relatively new phenomenon, fathers have been absent from family life in one way or another for many decades. Consequently, more attention has been given to this subject in looking for the possible effects on boys of lacking an available male role model. Girls were considered to be less affected. But there are many processes operating in family relationships, and many of the women writing to me who had 'lost' their fathers in some way were convinced that this absence had influenced them as much as their father's presence might have done.

As time passes, the ageing proces takes its toll and fathers may begin to affect their daughters' lives through their incipient physical vulnerability and potential dependency. The roles move into reverse and women begin to think protectively about their fathers. Illness can have mellowing effects on cantankerous old men whose impending confrontation with mortality drives their emotions into the foreground. A daughter may find herself having meaningful conversations with her father, from which they could both have benefited forty or fifty years earlier.

Although there was a wide age range in the daughters participating in this research, there was great similarity between many of the experiences described by older women looking back to their childhood and early adulthood and those of younger women describing their current situations. The passage of time reflected a relaxation in the role of fathers as strict patriarchs and upholders of the family's sexual morality, parallelling the lower importance that religion takes in many families today. This does not necessarily mean that young women now find it easier to talk with their fathers about personal issues than their own mothers did with their own fathers, but that there is a less formal atmosphere surrounding such subjects as boyfriends and sex. Where the cultural background defines a particularly strong patriarchal dominance, for example, in Asian and Cypriot families, this can still exert a strong influence. A proportion of young men and women in successive generations however, have developed less strict relationships.

Many factors – such as father's responses to female sexuality, the development of girls' autonomy and confidence, interpersonal communication and men's ability to express positive emotions – can cut across class divisions in father–daughter relationships. Researchers (usually middle-class) have tended to conclude that working-class families contain more aggression and violence than middle-class families. Such assumptions obscure the amount of threat and violence that can exist in middle-class homes, where violence may be expressed in different ways. The socio-economic conditions under which some families struggle to survive may also act as triggers for violence rather than some inherent 'class' factor. The only such class factor to emerge from the father–

daughter relationships involved here was that in some working-class families the daughter had shown herself more intelligent and achieving than her low-achieving father, whose response was to feel threatened and to be verbally or physically hurtful to his daughter. This was often in an atmosphere of intimidation in the family, which seemed to reflect a high level of male insecurity. But there were other working-class families in which fathers were very supportive and delighted to see their daughters achieve what they had not had the opportunity to do. It was the personality, background and upbringing of the fathers that determined their response to their daughters' success. Those fathers of any background who are confident in their own status will experience their daughters' success as a positive rather than negative reflection on themselves. For their part, daughters from working-class families who have taken higher educational opportunities have probably experienced greater social mobility since the Second World War than working-class boys.

Men as fathers hold power granted by their patriarchal role in the family and society, which gives them a physical, social and economic advantage in the father–daughter relationship in the early years, and sometimes far beyond. One disadvantage their role carries, however, is that (heterosexual) masculinity does not allow much space or status for emotions. Several other authors[1] writing about the father–daughter relationship have observed, as I have, men's relative inability to express feelings and emotions, their avoidance of the 'weakness' of vulnerability, and their reluctance to be physically or emotionally close. Society makes demands of men as fathers, and whether he wants it or not a father may find his role is often concentrated in defining and enforcing authority and discipline. There is a contradiction between maintaining an image of power and authority within the family, and becoming closer to children and showing feelings and other signs of emotional 'weakness'. This is not to say that men do not have such feelings but that they are often locked away. Positive ('feminine') expressions of emotions like sadness and joy conflict with the requirements of socially constructed masculinity. Where men's emotions may gain more acceptable expression is through aggression and sexuality. Violence and abuse can then become a pathological expression of emotions turned on to the family.

How then can we create boys and men who have a greater facility for positive emotional expression, and who will be different sorts of fathers to their own children? Part of the answer lies in redefining the role of the father, but this is not easy since the weight of the present socio-economic structure still places men in a patriarchal position and reinforces physical strength and power as male stereotypes. The nuclear family hangs on by a thread in western societies, but it is quite a strong thread and still represents an ideal. There have been changes in the nature of fathers and fathering, and significant movement from the strict Victorian stereotype to more casual parental relationships. In recent years this has been stimulated by some movement towards parents sharing domestic labour and childcare but, overall, these changes have been slow and small. The effects of family separation and lone parenting or split parenting have probably had the greatest effects on fathers, who have found themselves precipitated into levels of childcare responsibility they had never anticipated. Within the family, some parents have made conscious steps towards non-sexist child-rearing, and others have at least changed some of the assumptions they used to make about female gender roles. Girls themselves express many attitudes and expectations about domestic equality which are destined to conflict with those of the boys who may be their future partners.

Many fathers and daughters speaking in these pages gain much mutual pleasure from their relationship, often despite a context of conflict and family friction. There is, however, no blueprint nor set prescription that guarantees a good father–daughter relationship. Even when I found myself describing what these women and men thought about the 'ideal' father–daughter relationship and what makes a 'good' father, the characteristics they suggested – closeness and communication, for example – would enhance a relationship between any two people. General formulas can easily end up sounding like platitudes. Where fathers can be particularly important, it seems, is in propagating and sustaining a sense of confidence and independence in their daughters. This involves generating a warm and trusting relationship, within which a girl experiences the encouragement and expectation that she is equal to anything she wants to try, and is given enough space to develop her own separate identity. It is a lot easier to write this sentence than it is to create the relationship, but it can be done, and mainly through changes in men and fathering.

This book has explored some of the important factors and processes operating between fathers and daughters, from both sides of the relationship. They demonstrate a constantly changing dynamic which can range between positive and negative at different times during their lives. Fathers have a powerful effect on their daughters, sometimes enhancing, sometimes damaging. In the face of such damage, the capacity of women (and men) to resist and change gives good cause for optimism. With the passing years, there is still time for both fathers and daughters to make new discoveries about what is the first, may be the most significant, and is one of the longest relationships that a woman and a man may have together.

Glossary of daughters and fathers

Alice is sixteen. She is a dance and drama student living in the northwest of England. She has two older brothers and lives with her mother. She rarely sees either her real father or her stepfather since he and her mother split up.

Anne is thirty-one, single and the only child from her father's second marriage. She does advocacy work in London and her father, aged seventy-four, is a retired fireman.

Barbara is twenty-eight and the youngest of four sisters. She trained as a teacher, married and left work to look after her small daughter in the south of England. Her father **John** is seventy. He rebelled against entering the family business when he was young and went into farming instead.

Bridget is sixty-three and the youngest of two sisters. Her father, who worked on the docks, died when she was thirty.

Carole is thirty-five and is training to be a counsellor. She is divorced with a teenage daughter.

Diana is a thirty-six-year-old journalist. She and her five brothers and sisters grew up with her parents in Scotland where her father worked as a gardener.

Elaine is forty-four, single and a freelance ceramic artist working in the north of England. She is the eldest of three sisters. Her father, **Jim**, has always worked on the railways, moving from being 'greaser boy' to working in the ticket office.

Eve is forty-six and married with two children. Her father died a few years ago.

Fiona is twenty-eight, with two young children, living with her partner Ben in London. Her father **David** is a journalist in his mid-sixties. Fiona is the third of David's four daughters from three marriages.

Gill is twenty-three and a lone mother with a small son, living in London. Her father is in his forties, works as a photographer and lives with his second wife and small daugher.

Helen is a eighteen-year-old music student studying in London. Until recently she lived in southeast England with her father **Graham**, a music teacher in his early forties, and her mother and younger brother.

Jane is fifty-nine and a retired teacher. She has four brothers and sisters. Her father, a local government official, is no longer alive.

Jean is a twenty-year-old student living in Scotland. She has five brothers and sisters, most of whom have left home but, like her, visit their parents regularly. Her father is a retired foundry manager.

Judy is thirty-four and lives in northwest England with her two children and her second husband. She works as a teacher. Her father, a bricklayer, and her mother also live in northern England.

Kate is twenty-eight and works as a secretary in London. When she was young her parents had a newsagent's. Her father has recently been very ill.

Laura is fifteen and lives with her parents and eighteen-year-old brother in the northwest of England. Her father **Tony** has a managerial post with the Electricity Board.

Lesley is thirty-eight and has worked in a variety of short-term jobs, such as her current post with an AIDS information network. She is an only child. Her father, **Bob**, has a job with the Electricity Board and lives with Lesley's mother in the south of England.

Lisa is thirty and an only child. She grew up in northwest England with her father, a skilled manual worker, and her mother, a teacher.

Louise is a twenty-six-year-old art and drama graduate. She is single and works in a London office. She grew up with both parents and younger brother until her parents split up when she was sixteen. Her father **Ian** is a freelance consultant in his forties.

Malcolm is a freelance writer in his thirties who lives with his wife and thirteen-year-old daughter **Anna** in the southwest of England.

Maria is nineteen and from a Greek-Cypriot family living in London. She works as a secretary and is soon to be married to her fiancé Andy. They both currently live at home with her father and mother.

Margaret works in social research and lives with her second husband and children in the south of England. She and her sister, both now in their late thirties, come from a Jewish family. Her father **Raymond** worked as a self-employed businessman until he retired.

Maureen is thirty-two and one of three sisters. She is divorced from her husband and works as a temporary secretary. Her father worked as a patent agent. He later divorced her mother and remarried.

Meena is thirty-two and lives with her husband and two small children in the south of England. Her father, a painter and art teacher, came from Pakistan.

Melanie is fourteen and spends alternate weeks living in London with her mother and half-sister. The rest of the time she spends with her father **Peter**, a building maintenance worker studying surveying.

Michelle is seventeen and lives with her family in the east of England. Her father is the workshop manager in a garage.

Neil is a lone father in his late twenties caring for his five-year-old daughter **Emily** and three-year-old son. He does private tuition in the evenings so that he can look after the children during the day.

Olwen is thirty-seven and lives in Wales. Her father was in the navy when she was young and was consequently away from home for many weeks at a time.

Patrick and his partner Josie are both students who share the care of their four-year-old daughter **Ella**.

Paula aged fourteen, and eleven-year-old **Kim** live in London with **Tom**, a teacher in his forties. Their mother lives close by, but they spend most time with Tom, who is stepfather to Paula and father to Kim. Paula does not know her real father, who lives in Trinidad.

Rosemary is thirty-eight and pregnant with her first child. She works in conservation and lives with her partner Matthew in London. Her father, **Stanley**, a retired insurance salesman in his seventies, lives just north of London with his wife, Gwen.

Sally is thirty-one. Her parents split up in Barbados when she and her younger sister were small, and both parents remarried. Her father later separated and lives alone.

Sean is a college lecturer in his forties who has four children through three separate relationships. He works and lives alone in the southwest of England, but regularly visits his two small daughters in London.

Sheila is twenty-nine and lives in Wales with her husband and small daughter. Her father came to northern England from Ireland at seventeen where he married her mother and had five children, of whom Sheila is the eldest.

Shirley is forty-seven, single and works in a college of further education.

Sonia is in her late thirties, married with young children, and living with her husband in the north of England. She works as a neighbourhood officer. Her sixty-two-year-old father still works as a self-employed painter and decorator in the Midlands.

Sonika is a twenty-three-year-old secretary living in London. Two years ago she had an arranged marriage to her husband, who is thirty-two. Her father works as a carpenter: he is from India, her mother is from Kenya.

Sophie is a nineteen-year-old university student who usually lives at home in the West Country with her parents and her boyfriend Simon. Her father **Richard**, who is fifty-four, gave up work as a sales representative some years before to study history as a mature student.

Stella is forty-nine and has been married and divorced three times. Her father, now eighty-two, was in the army and therefore the family moved around the country a lot when she was young.

Wendy is in her late thirties and the eldest of three daughters. She worked in a bank, married at nineteen and had two sons. She is now divorced. Her father is sixty-two and came from Ireland when he was young to work in the car industry.

Yvonne is an only child who grew up with her parents in the north of England. Her elderly father has developed Alzehimers Disease.

Notes

INTRODUCTION

1 C. Lewis. in C. Lewis and M. O'Brien. *Fatherhood Reassessed*, London, Sage, 1987.
2 For example, Linda E. Boose and Betty S. Flowers (eds), *Daughters and Fathers*, Baltimore: The Johns Hopkins University Press, 1989; Signe Hammer, *Passionate Attachments: Fathers and Daughters in America Today*, New York, Rawson Associates, 1982; Victoria Secunda, *Women and their Fathers*, London, Cedar, 1993.
3 Ursula Owen (ed.). *Fathers: Reflections by Daughters*, London, Virago, 1983.
4 Linda Schierse Leonard. *The Wounded Woman: Healing the Father–Daughter Relationship*, Boston and London, Shambhala, 1982.
5 Sean French (ed.). *Fathering*, London, Virago, 1992, is one exception but many of the fathers included focus more on their experiences of fathering as sons, rather than as fathers themselves.
6 Victoria Secunda, op. cit., Note 2.

CHAPTER 1   LITTLE GIRLS

1 David Lynn looks at the evidence that suggests that the father tends to be the parent most concerned with sextyping. It must be noted that much of the psychological work on the effects of mothers and fathers on their sons or daughters was done many years ago and this kind of research will therefore reflect aspects of the social structure and ideology of the times. *The Father: His Role in Child Development*, Monterey, Cal., Brooks/Cole, 1974.
2 Brian Jackson, *Fatherhood*, London, Allen and Unwin, 1983.
3 Nancy Chodorow, *The Reproduction of Mothering*, Berkeley, University of California Press, 1978.
4 Such as John Bowlby, *Attachment and Loss*, London, Penguin, 1969. The evidence around maternal deprivation was reviewed in detail by Michael Rutter in *Maternal Deprivation Reassessed*, London, Penguin, 1972.

5 Sue Sharpe, *Double Identity: Lives of Working Mothers*, London, Penguin, 1984.
6 It is very hard to make any reliable and comparable measure of fathers' participation in childcare, as Lorna McKee describes in 'Fathers' participation in infant care: a critique', in Lorna McKee and Margaret O'Brien, *The Father Figure*, London, Tavistock, 1982.
7 This was illustrated in research I have done to update the findings of a study on girls at school, *Just Like A Girl*, London, Penguin, 1976, to be published in a new edition (forthcoming).
8 For example, in books such as Ann Oakley, *Sex, Gender and Society*, London, Temple Smith 1973; Sue Sharpe, *Just Like A Girl*, London, Penguin 1976; June Statham, *Daughters and Sons*, Oxford, Blackwell, 1986.
9 June Statham, op. cit. Note 8, discusses many relevant issues in the context of parents' experiences of trying to implement non-sexist childrearing.
10 David Lynn, op cit., Note 1.

CHAPTER 2   APPROVAL AND ACHIEVEMENT

1 Some of the daughters contributing to Judith Arcana's research also expressed these kinds of views, in *Our Mother's Daughters*, London, The Women's Press, 1981; David Lynn has also explored the idea that fathers and mothers have different modes of loving: mother's love is unconditional while father's love is more demanding and conditional on performance. Based on work done in the 1960s, it is perhaps more appropriate for boys than girls at that time. He also applies Talcott Parsons' theory of fathers having an instrumental role in the family while mothers have an expressive role. *The Father: His Role in Child Development*, Monterey, Cal., Brooks/Cole, 1974.
2 Judith Arcana, op. cit., Note 1.
3 Deborah Tannen, *You Just Don't Understand*, London, Virago, 1992.
4 Miriam Johnson describes research that shows high achievers having had a close, supportive and encouraging relationship with their fathers, but she warns against the risk that this is at the cost of achieving only to please men. She quotes the finding that such women who work in high positions are often unable to be assertive in their personal relationships: they can only do this if the men they are being assertive with approve of what they are being assertive about. *Strong Mothers: Weak Wives*, Berkeley, University of California Press, 1988.

CHAPTER 3   DOMINANCE AND VIOLENCE

1 Valerie Walkerdine and Helen Lucey describe similar expressions of aggression and violence between working-class and middle-class daughters and their mothers, in *Democracy in the Kitchen*, London, Virago, 1989.

2 David Lynn, *The Father: His Role in Child Development*, Monterey, Cal., Brooks/Cole, 1974.
3 There has been a wealth of literature and research into family violence, much of which is concerned with wife–battering. This includes: R.E. Dobash and R.P. Dobash, *Violence Against Wives*, New York, The Free Press and Macmillan, 1979; C. Guberman and M. Wolfe, *No Safe Place: Violence Against Women and Children*, Ontario, Canada, The Women's Press, 1985; Alice Miller, *For Your Own Good: Hidden Cruelty in Childrearing and the Roots of Violence*, London, Virago, 1987.
4 Judith Arcana observes daughters' tendencies to accept and excuse unreasonable behaviour in their fathers in the name of love. This was also noted with respect to the desire for approval. *Our Mother's Daughters*, London, The Women's Press, 1981.
5 The increased reporting of sexual abuse inside and outside the family has given rise to much research and writing on the subject. For example: Elizabeth Ward, *Father–Daughter Rape*, London, The Women's Press, 1984; Sylvia Fraser, *My Father's House*, Canada, Doubleday, 1987; Bea Campbell, *Unofficial Secrets*, London, Virago, 1988; Liz Kelly, *Surviving Sexual Violence*, Cambridge, Polity Press, 1988.

CHAPTER 4   SEXUALITY

1 J. Holland, Caroline Ramazanoglu and Sue Sharpe, *Wimp or Gladiator: Contradictions in Acquiring Masculine Sexuality*, London, The Tufnell Press, 1993.
2 Rachel Thomson and Sue Scott, *Learning About Sex: Young Women and the Social Construction of Sexual Identity*, London, The Tufnell Press, 1992.
3 Sue Lees, *Losing Out*, London, Hutchinson, 1986, and *Sugar and Spice*, London, Penguin, 1993.
4 Sue Sharpe, *Falling For Love: Teenage Mothers Talk*, London, Virago, 1987.
5 Miriam Johnson looks at the lack of consistent evidence around the development of lesbianism in *Strong Mothers: Weak Wives*, Berkeley, University of California Press, 1988.
6 These aspects of the father–daughter relationship are also described by Destine, a young Turkish-Cypriot woman in Sue Sharpe, *Voices From Home*, London, Virago, 1990.

CHAPTER 5   OTHER MEN IN HER LIFE

1 Victoria Secunda, *Women and their Fathers*, London, Cedar, 1993.
2 W.S. Appleton, *Fathers and Daughters: A Father's Powerful Influence on a Woman's Life*, London, Macmillan, 1982.
3 W.S. Appleton, op cit., Note 2.

4 In this context, eighteen-year-old Claire describes her experiences of anorexia three years previously as a reaction to her strict father, and in an effort to gain some control over her own life; in Sue Sharpe, *Voices From Home*, London, Virago, 1990.

CHAPTER 6   WAYS OF FATHERING

1 As described, for instance, in David Lynn, *The Father: His Role in Child Development*, Monterey, Cal., Brooks/Cole, 1974.
2 For example, E. Mavis Hetherington, 'Girls Without Fathers', *Psychology Today*, Del Mar, Cal., February 1973; Elyce Wakerman, *Father Loss: Daughters Discuss Growing Up Without A Father*, London, Piatkus, 1984.
3 See, for instance, J. Burgogne and D. Clark, 'From Father to Stepfather', in L. McKie and M. O'Brien, *The Father Figure*, London, Tavistock, 1982; Erica De'Ath, (ed.), *Stepfamilies: What Do We Know? What Do We Need To Know?* London, Significant Publications, 1993; Elizabeth Hodder, *Stepfamilies Talking*, London, Macdonald Optima, 1989.

CHAPTER 8   CONCLUDING THOUGHTS

1 For example, Judith Arcana, *Our Mothers' Daughters*, London, The Women's Press, 1981.

Bibliography

Arcana, Judith. *Our Mothers' Daughters*, London, The Women's Press, 1981.
Appleton W.S. *Fathers and Daughters: A Father's Powerful Influence on a Woman's Life*, London, Macmillan, 1982.
Boose, Linda E. and Flowers, Betty S. (eds). *Daughters and Fathers*, Baltimore: The Johns Hopkins University Press, 1989.
Bowlby, John. *Attachment and Loss*, London, Penguin, 1969.
Campbell, Bea. *Unofficial Secrets*, London, Virago, 1988.
Chodorow, Nancy. *The Reproduction of Mothering*, Berkeley, University of California Press, 1978.
De'Ath, Erica (ed.). *Stepfamilies: What Do We Know? What Do We Need to Know?*, London, Significant Publications, 1993.
Dobash, R.E. and Dobash, R.P. *Violence Against Wives*, New York, The Free Press and Macmillan, 1979.
Fraser, Sylvia. *My Father's House*, Canada, Doubleday, 1987.
French, Sean. (ed.). *Fathering*, London, Virago, 1992.
Guberman C. and Wolfe, M. *No Safe Place: Violence Against Women and Children*, Ontario, Canada, The Women's Press, 1985.
Hammer, Signe. *Passionate Attachments: Fathers and Daughters in America Today*, New York, Rawson Associates, 1982.
Heatherington, E. Mavis. 'Girls Without Fathers', *Psychology Today*, Del Mar, Cal., February 1973.
Hodder, Elizabeth. *Stepfamilies Talking*, London, Optima, 1989.
Holland, J., Ramazanoglu, C. and Sharpe, S. *Wimp or Gladiator: Contradictions in Acquiring Masculine Sexuality*, London, The Tufnell Press, 1993.
Jackson, Brian. *Fatherhood*, London, Allen and Unwin, 1983.
Johnson, Miriam. *Strong Mothers: Weak Wives*, Berkeley, University of California Press, 1988.
Kelly, Liz. *Surviving Sexual Violence*, Cambridge, Polity Press, 1988.
Lees, Sue. *Losing Out*, London, Hutchinson, 1986.
Lees, Sue. *Sugar and Spice*, London, Penguin, 1993.
Leonard, Linda Schierse. *The Wounded Woman: Healing the Father–Daughter Relationship*, Boston and London, Shambhala, 1982.
Lewis, C. in C. Lewis, and M. O'Brien. *Fatherhood Reassessed*, London, Sage, 1987.

Lynn, David. *The Father: His Role in Child Development*, Monterey, Cal., Brooks/Cole,1974.

McKee, Lorna. 'Participation in infant care: a critique', in Lorna McKee and Margaret O'Brien, *The Father Figure*, London, Tavistock, 1982.

Miller, Alice. *For Your Own Good: Hidden Cruelty in Childrearing and the Roots of Violence*, London, Virago, 1987.

Oakley, Ann. *Sex, Gender and Society*, London, Temple Smith 1973.

Owen, Ursula. (ed.). *Fathers: Reflections by Daughters*, London, Virago, 1983.

Secunda, Victoria. *Women and Their Fathers*, London, Cedar, 1993.

Sharpe, Sue. *Just Like A Girl*, London, Penguin, 1976.

Sharpe, Sue. *Double Identity: Lives of Working Mothers*, London, Penguin, 1984.

Sharpe, Sue. *Falling For Love: Teenage Mothers Talk*, London, Virago, 1987.

Sharpe, Sue. *Voices From Home*, London, Virago, 1990.

Statham, June. *Daughters and Sons*, Oxford, Blackwell, 1986.

Tannen, Deborah. *You Just Don't Understand*, London, Virago, 1992.

Thomson, Rachel and Scott, Sue. *Learning About Sex: Young Women and the Social Construction of Sexual Identity*, London, The Tufnell Press, 1992.

Wakerman, Elyce. *Father Loss: Daughters Discuss Growing up without a Father*, London, Piatkus.

Walkerdine, Valerie and Lucey, Helen. *Democracy in the Kitchen*, London, Virago, 1989.

Ward, Elizabeth. *Father–Daughter Rape*, London, The Women's Press, 1984.

Index